Sting of the Heat Bug

Jack Sheedy

Sting of the Heat Bug
by Jack Sheedy

Signalman Publishing
www.signalmanpublishing.com
email: info@signalmanpublishing.com
Kissimmee, Florida

Cover design by Rob Cheney

Author photo by Jean Sands

ISBN: 978-1-935991-88-5 (paperback)
978-1-935991-89-2 (ebook)

Library of Congress Control Number: 2012953552

SIGNALMAN
PUBLISHING

For my wife, Jean Sands,
who lights my way

In a dark time, the eye begins to see…
—Theodore Roethke, "In a Dark Time"

What do you see when you turn out the light?
I can't tell you, but I know it's mine.
—The Beatles, "With a Little Help from My Friends"

1

What I do see is a memory of a memory, a hazy view from the bottom of a staircase when I am two years old. I am in a street-level apartment in a duplex near the Torrington Company. The pounding on the ceiling is scaring me, and it is scaring my three-year-old sister Peggy and my infant sister Ann. We are all crying, and Ann's colicky wailings are the loudest.

"Mommy, it's loud, what is it?" Peggy whines.

"Roud," I echo.

Mom is pacing, cradling Ann in her left arm. "John, where's the bottle?" she is asking my father.

CRASH! POUND! POUND!

A woman's voice on the big Philco radio is singing something about buttons and bows. "It's coming, Marion, it's all right," Dad is saying in as soothing a voice as he can manage. With a quick glance at the ceiling, he half stumbles, half shuffles out of the yellow-wallpapered kitchen, turning the glass baby bottle upside-down to test a drop of warm milk on his wrist.

"Oh, just let me." Mom takes the bottle, as Ann's cries get even louder. Mom's straight black hair hangs in her face.

KA-BOOM! CRASH! POUND!

"Mommy!" Peggy says.

"Mommy!" I say, because Peggy does.

"Shush, now," Mom says, looking at no one. Is she talking to me? To Peggy? Or to Ann?

"Oh dear, now what did I do?" Dad says. (Oh, it was to Dad.)

BOOM BOOM BOOM! POUND POUND POUND!

"I'm not talking to you!" Mom says to Dad, and Ann wails louder.

"Why is it noise up there?" Peggy says.

"Noise up air?" I repeat.

"John, can you take care of it, just this time?" Mom says, as if this happens every day. (Maybe it does. This is, after all, my earliest memory.)

"Daddy, what is it?" Peggy asks.

"It's nothing," he says, scooping us both up in his arms at once. Ann is now quiet, sucking on the bottle, and Mom has taken her into a bedroom. "There are two grownups up there, up those stairs, and one of them just fell off a chair, that's all."

"How they fell off a chair?" Peggy wants to know, and, now that she brings it up, so do I.

"Now there's a story," he says, and he settles himself onto the brown davenport with a child on each knee. His black eyebrows arch up as though he is amazed at our interest. It is late afternoon, and sunlight catches his eyeglasses, throwing a reflection onto the cracked plaster ceiling. Ann offers one last brief cry from the bedroom, and then is quiet. I wait for the ceiling to shake again, but it doesn't. A man's voice on the radio is saying, "And today, three years after the Enola Gay dropped …" before Dad reaches over and flicks it off. A wooden, round-topped clock on the mantle is ticking.

"Do you want to hear the story?" he says.

"Is it a daydream?" Peggy asks.

"Day deam?" I ask.

"It's a daydream," Dad says. "Just let me adjust this first." He reaches into his vest pocket and turns a tiny dial on a shiny metal box clipped there. A braided beige wire runs from the box to a black button in his ear. A squealing noise comes from his ear, and he winces and turns the dial again, then pokes at the black ear button until the squealing stops.

"Once upon a time," he begins, "there was a nice young man and a nice young woman with three young children named Peggy, Jack and Ann. They lived downstairs from an old man and an old woman in a house by the side of the road. One day, when it was hot and the children were crying …"

The ticking of the clock is soothing and rhythmic, and the oval ghost of light dances on the ceiling. Outside, diapers hang on a rope with wooden clothespins, waving slightly in an August afternoon breeze. Peggy's eyes close first, and Dad's voice goes on and on, and I think it must go on and on even after my own eyes close.

2

What I really remember is the view of the staircase, the constant pounding on the ceiling, and sepia-toned images of Mom and Dad and Peggy in that small apartment. Peggy or I ask what it is. "Someone fell off a chair," either Mom or Dad says.

Years later, when I'm eight or nine, I ask Mom if that really happened, or if I imagined it. "Oh, all the time," she says, playing a red three on a black four. "Nobody fell off a chair, though. We used to tell you kids that, but it was really the landlady upstairs, banging on her floor to keep you kids quiet. That's why we moved."

This news upsets me. "You mean it wasn't real? What I saw? What I heard? It didn't happen?"

She doesn't answer, because of course I don't really ask that. It's just something that I wish I had asked, and so I've made it part of my life story, just like I made the yellow wallpaper, the baby bottle, the voices on the radio, the diapers on the line, and the daydream part of my first view from the bottom of the stairs. They could have happened.

When I am—let's say I am ten—Dad takes me to a boat show in Hartford. I don't even know why, since as far as I know there is never any chance we are going to buy a boat. We stand in front of a fourteen-foot aluminum sailboat, admiring the lines. When we get home, Dad tells Mom we have seen a forty-foot brass-trimmed cruiser with twin inboard motors, air-conditioned dining area and a roomy double-bed cabin. "We didn't see a boat like that," I say.

"You have to embellish when you tell a story," he whispers.

Actually, I think it was a car show. No matter.

No matter, too, that some of the names in this book are changed, and some are not. No matter that some events are like an alarm clock I once disassembled when I was maybe seven and got pretty much back together, except for a couple of springs and two screws; the clock was incomplete, but it kept good time.

Now Peggy and I are on a shelf, gazing at clouds through the rear window of Mom's 1940 black Ford coupe. Dad is driving, Mom is bottle-feeding Ann, and Dad is leading us in song. "There's a tree in Pine Meadow-ww!" he sings, to the tune of a song I've never heard since, and Mom joins in. We are in the country, away from city streets and close-together houses, and we're pulling into a dirt driveway. The white stucco house looks like a castle, sitting by itself with two giant, now leafless, fountain-shaped willow trees hanging over the sun porch, and big barnlike buildings attached to the back. Rainspouts from the roof lead to big wooden barrels.

We run through the house, exploring. There's a chipped-ceramic, white Glenwood gas stove, a pantry with a double sink for washing dishes, a door to a stairway that goes down, as well as one that goes up. Dad goes down the cellar stairs and invites Peggy and me to follow. "Hold onto the banisters," he says, introducing a new word to our vocabularies. They are big white wooden railings, and we have to reach up to hold onto them. There is a big machine that Dad says is a pump, and it makes a loud motor noise every few minutes, because Mom is turning faucets on and off in the pantry and bathroom.

"It's ours!" Dad shouts, standing outside the two-story former farmhouse. Eight rooms! Kitchen, dining room, living room, den, and four bedrooms. We have a house!"

"No more landlord!" Mom says, and Ann begins to wail.

"Go ahead, Ann," Dad says. "Cry! Cry as loud as you like! Cry your eyes out! Everybody, cry! This is a happy day!"

3

Now I'm three, and Mom has been missing for almost a week. It's six months after our move to the stucco house in the Puddletown section of New Hartford. A big woman is home with us during the day, in Mom's place, while Dad is working. Finally the 1940 Ford pulls into the driveway, with Dad driving, and the big woman tells Peggy and me to come outside to see our brother. Mom is in the passenger seat holding a pink baby. His name is Thomas Robert.

When I'm four, this happens again. This time, I know it's coming, and when Mom is about seven months pregnant, in July 1950, her stomach bulges way out when she sits in the living room chair. "It's kicking," she tells me. "Want to feel it?" I put my hand on her stomach and feel my brother Gerald Francis banging to get out early.

He succeeds. Mom falls in the backyard and delivers him a month ahead of schedule. Again the long days away from home, and again the same big woman watching Peggy and Ann and Tom and me. This time when the Ford pulls in with the new brother, even Ann toddles out with Peggy and me to gape at him. I start to think that more and more brothers and sisters will eventually join us in this ritual, until a dozen or more of us can swarm out of the house to see each new arrival. But Mom is closing in on age thirty-nine, and she has no intentions of having more babies, no matter what Pope Pius XII may think about the matter.

One day, I flush the toilet and water overflows. Have I flushed Gerald's diaper down again without thinking? Not this time. The septic tank is full. Dad starts digging in the backyard, and a septic cleaning truck pulls into the driveway. A sunburned man with no shirt helps Dad dig, and they pull a heavy round cement cover off the cesspool.

"There's your problem," the man says, pointing to milky bubbles floating in the muck.

"What are they?" Dad asks.

The man looks sideways at Dad. "Don't you know?"

"No."

"Rubbers."

"Can't be. We use galoshes."

"Not those kind. Safeties. Trojans. Condoms. Prophylactics. You know."

"Well, how did they get there?" Dad asks.

"You don't know?"

Peggy and I are standing near the apple tree nearby, watching. Ann and Tom are in a playpen near us. Mom is holding Gerald in her arms. Dad waves an arm dramatically to encompass all of us and says, "What do *you* think? I bought this house from a Frenchman. Evidently, he left something behind."

4

"You may go as far from home as you like," Dad tells Peggy and me. He is straightening a blue necktie, using a two-slice Toastmaster toaster as a mirror. He shoots his cuffs and twists blue-and-silver cufflinks onto the ends of white sleeves. His shoes are shiny black Oxfords, his pants charcoal gray wool. A matching charcoal suit jacket hangs on the back of a green vinyl-padded, chrome-legged kitchen chair. Last night's *Hartford Times* is folded back to the comics page, featuring his favorites, Ferdinand and Henry, who never speak. He is about to drive to his hearing aid office, which he calls Radioear of Hartford.

"We're not in Torrington any more," he says, sipping coffee and smearing Imperial margarine on his Wonder Bread toast. "No more city streets, no more harnessing Jack into a high chair on the porch. No more worrying that Peggy will push Ann's stroller into oncoming traffic like she almost did on James Street. We're in the country now, and you're free to roam."

"Almost free," Mom puts in, looking up from mixing flour, milk and eggs with a hand-cranked rotary beater. "You can't cross the road or the tracks. And you can't get out of earshot."

This is considerably more limiting than Dad's "as far from home as you like," but we accept it. Route 44, the old Albany Turnpike, is a much busier thoroughfare than James Street ever was or will be. It is the main road to Hartford, some twenty-five miles to the southeast, and it meanders northwest into fairly well-populated Winsted, where factories draw commuter traffic as well as delivery truck traffic. Our house is on the outside of a bend. A wooded embankment that spills from the inside of the curve blocks visibility in both directions.

"You can go in either direction north or south, but never cross the road or the tracks," Dad says to us, shooting Mom a quick, impatient glance. "Am I explaining this, or are you?" he says to her.

"Well, it's not what we discussed," she says. She dips her hand in a glass of water and shakes droplets onto the skillet. The skillet hisses.

"I'm getting to it," Dad says. "I don't want them to feel—"

"You can't say they can go wherever they want and then say they can't," she says. She is ladling a pale yellow circle of batter onto the skillet, and the circle widens and widens.

"I'm not hungry," Peggy says. "I don't want any pancakes."

"I do!" I say. "I love pancakes."

"No, Jack, come on," Peggy says.

"But I'm hungry," I say.

"You'll both stay and eat breakfast," Mom says.

Dad drains his coffee cup and carries it and the saucer and spoon to the pantry sink. "All right," he says softly to Peggy. "Do what your mother says." He kisses his six-year-old daughter on the cheek and puts his suit jacket over his arm. He looks at me. "Give me a kiss, Jack, I've got no favorites!" he says with a grin.

Then he is out the door, carrying a black bag filled with hearing aid tools.

Mom is silently filling our plates with pancakes. She goes to the Frigidaire and gets Caro syrup, places it near the margarine.

"All right, there you are," she says. "Butter or maple syrup?" she asks. Of course, both choices are ersatz, but she still calls them butter and maple syrup.

"I'll have syrup today," Peggy says.

"I'll have both," I say.

"One or the other," Mom says. "You can't have both."

"Can we go see Mr. Bills?" Peggy asks.

"After breakfast," Mom says. "He's within earshot, right next door."

"Or maybe we can visit Minnie Hough," Peggy says, exploring the limits of her freedom.

"All right," Mom says. "Minnie and George are within earshot in the other direction."

"Can we walk to Mr. Bills's spring in the woods?" Peggy says.

"No, that's across the street."
"Can we go down to the river?"
"No, that's across the tracks."
"Me and Jack are going to see—"
"Jack and I," Mom says.
"Jack and I are going to see Mr. Bills," Peggy announces.

I take the syrup, and I take a lot of it. When Mom isn't looking I take the margarine, too.

5

We are walking across the strawberry patch, Peggy in the lead, trudging the trail that divides the patch into two sections. She walks confidently, munching on Hostess Cupcakes she sneaked from the bread box after refusing the pancakes, and I marvel at how tall she is, even though for forty-eight days of every year we are the same age. Her hair, long and black, hangs straight down to her shoulders. When she turns around to tell me to hurry up, the sun peeking over the hills to the east lights up her hazel eyes. Her black eyebrows arch up just like Dad's when she says, "Well, come on, slowpoke!"

I follow my sister, because she is my whole world. Ann is only three years and two months old, sullen and thumbsucking, an intruder into our world. Tom is two years and a month, and Gerald is ten months old. Peggy and I, ages six and five, are practically grownups in comparison.

"I'm coming," I say. "Don't go so fast."

"Well, we're never gonna get there," she says.

It is eight o'clock on a Saturday morning in June 1951, and Mr. Bills's house is a twenty-two-second walk through the strawberry patch, but to hear Peggy talk it will be nightfall by the time we reach it. I bend down to pick a ripe strawberry that lies in the path.

"Don't pick that!" she says. "Let's go!"

I bite into the berry, spitting out dirt and chewing down to the leafy stem, getting it all. Peggy has turned around to face me with her hands on her hips.

"Hurry up!" she says.

I don't know why I am holding back. If Peggy had suddenly turned and said, "All right, let's go home," I would put up a fuss.

The buzzing noise starts up, the high-in-a-tree noise from an unseen cicada, and we both look up toward the remnants of an apple orchard on the edge of the railroad tracks. The droning grows louder and then stays at a steady pitch and volume, and the whole world stands still. It seems to cover the morning with noise, insisting that we listen until it starts to fade away.

"What is it?" I ask.

"It's the heat bug," Peggy says. "Mom told me."

"What does it look like?"

"You can't see it. It's in-visitable."

"How do you know?"

"Mom told me."

"How does Mom know?"

"She knows."

"Does it sting?"

"I don't know. Yes. Mom says it stings."

"She did not."

"She did so. But if you don't bother it, it doesn't sting."

"That's bees and wasps," I say.

"Well, heat bugs, too, Mom says."

"If you can't see it, how do you know when you're bothering it?"

"Because it stings," she says.

Mr. Bills's house is a big, boxy duplex covered with fake maroon bricks made of tarpaper. Old Mr. Bills lives upstairs with fat Bertha Atkins, who runs the Tydol gas station and luncheonette a few steps farther south. She is the woman who babysat when Mom went to the hospital to get my baby brothers. The downstairs part of the house is for Mr. Bills's carpentry workshop and cider storage. But the big attraction for Peggy and me is the house he has been building on the property since before we moved here, banging a nail now and then when he has the lumber and ambition between drunks.

The house is still a skeleton of light brown timbers, with squares left empty for windows and doors and a triangle of boards for a roof peak. Inside we can see vertical boards where walls will go and a zigzag that will one day be a staircase. It's like looking through the skin of a house and seeing the whole thing at once, inside and out. Years later, when it is all finished, I will look at it from across the strawberry patch and know just where the bedrooms and closets are.

"Hi, Mr. Bills!" Peggy shouts.

He is fifty-eight years old, bent over a sawhorse, rhythmically sawing a floorboard to fit in the corner of the future living room, by a future picture window. He squints up at us, red-faced, grinning, a blue denim baseball cap shading his eyes. He looks down at his work and mumbles something.

"What?" Peggy says.

"I said, 'Come out of the sun,'" he says. "Go, stand in the shade of the big house until I'm done. Are you thirsty?"

"I am!" I say, knowing he has a big vat of cold water fed by a spring that runs through a pipe under the road.

Peggy turns around. "Quiet," she says.

Mr. Bills grins and takes his cap off, wipes his face with it. A hammer hangs from a loop in his torn blue overalls, and a stubby pencil points at us from above his right ear.

"Well, go on in and take a drink of water," he says. "Peggy, take your brother in to get a drink."

He bends back to his work and sneaks a quick glance at us to see if we're obeying him. Peggy and I walk in the open door of the duplex where Mr. Bills keeps ladders and worktables and tools. Water from a spigot is constantly pouring into a black iron vat as tall as Peggy. It is always full, and the overflow pipe leads to the outside where it irrigates the strawberry patch. Peggy and I stand on an upside-down wooden Coca-Cola crate from Bert's Tydol station.

"You first," Peggy says.

"No, you."

"Both together, then, but be careful. Remember last time."

"He's outside," I say.

"OK, both together," Peggy says.

We dip our mouths into the sweet, icy water and drink long and deep. It is so cold and refreshing that we don't want to stop. I come up for air once and see Peggy still drinking. Then she comes up for air and I drink again, and Peggy joins me, and we drink and drink.

SPLOOSH! Our heads are pushed deep into the frigid water and held there for two or three seconds. I feel a rough hand on the back of my head as water fills my nose and throat, and I squirm free. Peggy is free now too and gasping for air, swinging her arms at Mr. Bills, who is laughing.

"Ahahaha! I gotcha again!" he says.

"Don't do that!" Peggy screams.

I am coughing and snorting, clearing my sinuses. "I could drownd!" I shout. "You could drownd us!"

"Ah, you won't drown, I just dunked you for a second, all in fun," Mr. Bills says. "All right, come on outside and help me build the house."

Back outside in the sun, I hear the invisible heat bug start up again, and I'm afraid it will sting me when I'm not looking.

6

Mr. Bills hobbles back to the workshop to answer the telephone. "Two rings, that's me," he says, mussing my hair as he brushes past me. While he is inside, Peggy squeezes between support beams and is inside the skeleton of the house. "I'm in, you're out!" she taunts. "Here's the kitchen, where I'm baking apple pies, like Mom. Here's the room where a sick person is dying, and I'm taking care of him, like Mom does."

"You can't go in there," I say.

"I'm already in."

"Mr. Bills says not to."

"He says not to go near the stairs, and I'm not. You can stay there if you want."

I do, for now, but I can see Peggy pretending to be interested in the BX-cables, the sawdust on the plank floors, the pencil marks on the freshly cut boards. She sneaks a glance at me every few seconds, but I stay put.

I am looking at a cardboard box that has four flaps folded into each other so that half of each flap is under half of its neighboring flap. The pattern is fascinating. I mentally try folding an imagined box. Fold one flap down, then fold the next one over it and fold the third one over the second one. Now for the fourth and final flap: How do you get half of the last flap under half of the first flap without bending the cardboard? I lose myself in the puzzle for maybe five minutes.

"Away from the stairway!" Mr. Bills shouts at Peggy. He hustles past me, nails jingling in his overalls pockets.

"I'm not near—"

"You were close enough," he says, picking her up from behind in a sort of bear hug and laughing as he carries her back outside. He tickles her under the arms briefly and chuckles when Peggy squirms and laughs helplessly.

"Well, that was your mother," he says. "Sounds like you're having strawberry shortcake tonight. I told her she could pick as many strawberries as she needs."

Sure enough, we hear the spring-loaded screen door of our sun porch slam shut, and there's Mom in a red-and-white blouse and white shorts and sandals, carrying a large saucepan. She sees us from across the strawberry patch and waves to us.

"OK, Jack boy," Mr. Bills says. "Hand me that saw, can you do that? We're gonna finish those stairs."

Peggy wanders away to help Mom pick strawberries, and Mr. Bills lets me pound a few nails into stair treads. My mind wanders, and I pick up a bent nail and trace patterns in the sawdust.

"You're no carpenter," Mr. Bills says. "Better git 'fore you hurt yourself. Go on, help your Mom pick berries."

I join Mom and Peggy and start pulling at half-ripe berries that crush in my hands. Mom tells me I'm no farmer and sends me home.

Peggy comes home ahead of Mom. "Hey, there's ants," she says, suddenly squatting in the dirt driveway. I join her and watch, enthralled at the seemingly endless numbers of tiny creatures emerging from a small mound of sand.

Peggy is the first to hear the tractor, and she knows immediately what it means. "Look, Johnny Ryan is coming!"

An old, rust-red Ford tractor is chugging along the side of the road toward our house, driven by seventy-four-year-old Johnny Ryan, who lives a mile south of us. He doesn't look at us, just swerves his tractor into our property and begins turning over the dirt in Mom's garden with a rust-colored assortment of clanging metal wheels. He is finished in less time than it takes him to drive to our house, and he leaves immediately, never once uttering a word or stopping his tractor. This is the third year in a row that he has plowed Mom's garden, and he will continue plowing it every year for another ten years.

Peggy and I go back to watching the ants quietly turning our driveway inside out. "What happens when ants get old?" Peggy asks.

"I guess they just die," I say.

"But before that, what? Do they keep carrying dirt out of the hole until they die? Or do they get tired and stop working? Do the other ants take care of them?"

"How should I know?" I am surprised that my older sister would seek answers from me.

"Well, I don't want to watch ants die. Let's go down cellar and clap the whites," she says.

I follow her into the house and down the cellar stairs.

"It's just the right time of day," she says. "And it's sunny."

She leads me to the narrow cellar window on the south side, near the coal furnace, where sunlight is streaming into the dark cellar. Millions of dust motes are swimming in the sunbeam like a miniature blizzard. Peggy reaches into the light and claps her hands.

"Got one!" she says, as the motes swirl faster.

I reach in and clap. "Me too!"

"Did not!"

"Did too!"

The screen door bangs shut upstairs. Mom calls us up. "Wash your hands and help me," she says.

"I helped you pick," Peggy says. "Do I have to?"

"All right, Jack," Mom says.

Peggy sticks her tongue out at me and goes into the living room to color.

Mom shows me how to take the leafy stems off without squishing the berries, and when the job is done, she says I can eat one. "Wash it first, then eat just one. There's just enough for shortcake." She puts the berries in a colander and rinses them in the pantry sink and places the colander in the saucepan to drain. "I'm going to the garden," she says. "I didn't get Johnny Ryan to plow until today, and I need to start planting pole beans or we won't have any later this summer."

The one berry she said I could eat was perfectly juicy and sweet. But there is still a heaping mound of identical berries. Dad is working. Peggy and the other siblings are playing elsewhere. Mom is in the garden. I am hungry.

I am about to discover the perfect crime: an illegal act that forever goes undetected and unpunished, and yet profits the perpetrator. It is impossible to tell if one strawberry is missing from a mound of several hundred. I take one and eat it, and no change to the pile is evident. So I take another one. Still no change. I take five more, each one at a time, and there is no discernible change each time I take one. Later that night, we have strawberry shortcake, and there is plenty for seven people. I even have seconds.

7

"First two couples for'd an' back, for'd again, cross over!" This is how I can tell it's a Saturday. George Hough, the sixtyish neighbor to our north, is pushing a mechanical lawn mower on a sweaty July day, a can of Rheingold beer in one hand as the mower blades go clacketa-clacketa-clacketa. He is wearing brown shorts and a low-slung undershirt, showing off skinny legs and white chest hair. He is calling an imaginary square dance.

"Dip your partner an' a do-si-do, hook those arms, go round an' round!"

The Houghs' white clapboard house is even closer to ours than Mr. Bills's house, just a row of pole beans away through Mom's vegetable garden. Here in our own yard, Dad is pushing the bottom of a teardrop-shaped oil can as drops of amber oil coat the wheels of his own mower. It makes a hollow plunka-plunka sound. He looks over at George and says to me, "Tell your mother I'm going next door."

Words are still only auditory vibrations to me, since I won't be reading until I'm seven. The expression always sounds like "neck store," and I wonder vaguely if the Houghs are selling chicken necks or something from their woodshed.

"Can I come to the neck store too?" I say.

He considers. "Well, why not? Let's go see Minnie and George."

Dad grabs a fresh bottle of Miller High Life from a metal wash tub filled with ice. Then he grabs a second bottle, checks to see if his opener is in his pocket, and says, "Let's go, Jack."

"Men step left and ladies step right, swing that new girl all the way round!"

"George, what's the word?" Dad says, clapping George on the back, startling him.

"Who's that? Hey, put your dukes up!" he says, feigning a John L. Sullivan pose and dancing clumsily.

"George, it's only John, your neighbor," Dad says soothingly.

"Aw, John, I know that," George says. "I'm just funning. You got that beer for me?"

"Sure, if you've got a bottle opener," Dad says.

"Aw, John, my church key's in the kitchen, I don't want to go in there now, Minnie's cooking. I'm nursing this little bit of Rheingold."

"How many have you had?" Dad asks.

"Just one. It don't take much, John! Hey, swing your partner with a— who's that?" he says suddenly, looking at me.

Dad gathers me to him by my shoulder. "It's my son Jack, George, you know him."

"Put your dukes up, Jack!" He dances backwards, forearms guarding his face, trips over his foot and falls on his back.

"I'm all right," he says, scrambling immediately to his feet. Minnie comes bustling out of the house, and the back porch screen door squawks and slams behind her. She is a round woman wearing a faded green house dress and a white apron. She is carrying a half-peeled potato that trails a foot-long strip of brown skin.

"George, you settle down now," she says in a nasal whine. Her voice somehow reminds me of the taste of green apples, but I can never explain why.

"Aw, Minnie, don't holler on me!" George says. "Hey, first two couples!"

"It's all right, Minnie," Dad says. "He was just doing a pratfall for Jack, to make him laugh."

No one notices that I'm not laughing.

"You just be careful, then," Minnie says, walking back to the house, potato peel flapping.

"Here, George, I've got an opener," Dad says.

"Aw, John, why'd you ask if I had a church key then?" George says.

"Minnie told me your limit is two. After that, she takes the opener from you."

"John, I swear I've just had the one. I just left the opener inside. Here, hand me that thing, I'll open it."

George fusses for a few seconds before realizing he's trying to use the wrong end. He turns it around and finally sprays open the bottle of Miller.

"Thanks, John. You've got the high-class beer, hey?"

"The champagne of bottled beer," Dad says, wiping foam from his eyeglasses.

"Nothin' wrong with Rheingold, though," George says.

"I've got Rheingold in my Frigidaire," Dad says, though I know he just has Miller and Knickerbocker.

Minnie comes running out again, shaking a potato peeler. "George, you put that down, you've had your limit!" she whinnies.

"Aw, Minnie!"

"No, you just finish mowing the lawn. I'm sorry, John, he's had two beers already, hee-hee!" she says with a nervous giggle.

"Is he drunk?" I say.

Everybody stares at me.

Minnie finally speaks. "No, Jack, hee-hee, he's just a little cuckoo, that's all. Just cuckoo. He doesn't get drunk."

"First two couples an' a—no, dip your partner. Aw, Minnie, now you made me forget it all!" George says.

8

Nothing makes me sadder than hearing Peggy cry. When Ann or Tom or Gerald cries, it's an irritant, an interruption to my reveries, a noise I want to stifle. But when Peggy cries, my own world is at stake. Like the drone of the heat bug, the wailing is unceasing and all-involving. I sit on the fifth tread from the bottom of the staircase and peer through the banister's vertical pickets as Mom picks Peggy up and hugs her.

"Daddy will drive you to school," Mom says. It is Peggy's first day of second grade, and she has missed the bus.

"He said I have to walk!" Peggy says between sobs that make my own chest hurt.

"Oh, nonsense, you don't walk almost two miles along Route 44 all alone when you're six years old. He'll drive you. He doesn't think sometimes."

"But he'll be mad at me!"

"Pay kie-ing," says three-year-old Ann from inside the playpen at the top of the stairs. "Peggy crying," she means. Then she sits and puts her thumb in her mouth and starts whimpering herself, and I want to hit her.

"Shh!" I say, and Ann puts her head down on the mat, still sucking her thumb.

Floorboards creak as Dad opens the door to his and Mom's bedroom near the playpen. He puts the black hearing aid bag down and bends over to kiss Ann, then sees me on the stairs.

"You'd better get dressed," he says.

I walk upstairs and sit on my bed. I hear muffled voices downstairs. Peggy has stopped crying. Mom says something, then Dad answers immediately. Then I don't hear anything for a while, and finally Mom says something. A minute later, the kitchen door closes and I look out the upstairs window. Dad and Peggy are walking to the car.

I am still sitting on the bed twenty minutes later, wondering what to do. Mom has been tending to Tom and Gerald downstairs and now comes up to feed and change Ann. She sees me and says, "Your father told you to get dressed, I heard him."

"There's nothing to do," I say.

"Get dressed, that's something to start with," she says with no patience. "Then find something to eat."

I get my pants on easily enough, but the blue-and-white-striped jersey is on backwards and Mom skins the rabbit and manhandles me into it the right way. "Where are your socks?" she says. "You're supposed to put them on before your pants."

"I get them on wrong."

"Well, try."

"But the bumps end up on top all the time."

"Oh, just let me," she says, expertly rolling the socks up my leg.

Downstairs she shoves a piece of toast at me and tells me to go out and play. I walk into the sun porch and peel paint from the windowsills. Then I sit on the doorstep and gaze at the traffic on Route 44. Inside, Gerald is crying for his bottle. There is nothing to do out here, and I don't want to listen to crying inside.

I walk to one of the two big willow trees and peel bark off it. Then I sit on the low stone wall at the edge of the driveway and watch the Lyn Gas trucks go up and down the driveway the company shares with us as a right-of-way. One driver waves and asks, "Where's your sister I always see you with?"

"In school," I say. He drives on toward the propane plant across the railroad tracks.

Now I walk into the garage, which used to be a barn, and I walk through the side door to what was once a one-horse or one-cow stable. A ladder leads to a hayloft, but I don't go up there today.

Back outside, I walk down to the railroad tracks in the backyard. A diesel locomotive has just pushed a propane car onto a rail spur at the Lyn Gas building and is now backing the freight train onto the New York, New Haven & Hartford tracks again. The train gives a whistle and starts to gather speed as it passes our house. The engineer is wearing a white-and-blue-striped hat, almost the color of my jersey, and he waves to me. I wave back.

There is some hammering from Mr. Bills and what Dad calls "his never-ending project neck store," but I have no desire to go over there today. George Hough is standing on the side of the road with a lunch pail, waiting for a co-worker to give him a ride to the Collins Axe Company in Collinsville. He is neatly dressed in blue pants and shirt, and he doesn't look at all cuckoo today. He waves to me as his ride slows down to pick him up.

I go inside and ask Mom what time it is. She says it is about nine o'clock. I ask if it's time for lunch yet. She says no.

I find coals near the edge of the tracks and put them in the bed of my red toy dump truck. I sit in the shade of the willow trees and push the dump truck back and forth for hours, because I don't know what else to do.

From somewhere high in a tree across the tracks, a phoebe lifts its two-note call. It sounds like, "Peg-gy!" I squint precisely at the source of the sound, but I do not see the bird.

I linger over tomato soup and a baloney sandwich when Mom finally calls me for lunch. Tom and Gerald are napping, but now Ann is whimpering in her playpen. I go in the living room and color for a while. Then I go down cellar and watch the dust motes swimming in a sunbeam through the coal chute. Then I go upstairs and take a nap.

I wake to the sound of air brakes outside the house. I run to the window. A yellow school bus has opened its doors. I run downstairs, all excited. "Peggy's home!" I shout. "Peggy's home! Can I go out and play with Peggy?"

9

The Nickersons live just past the Tydol station. It's out of earshot, but in October 1951, Peggy and I can visit them because we'll be inside, watching Howdy Doody on their new Sylvania Television. Howdy Doody is always smiling, but when the unseen puppeteer manipulates the strings that make him lower his gaze and shake his head, I could swear the marionette's expression changes. "I don't know, Buffalo Bob," Howdy's voice says gravely. I forget what is bothering Howdy today—maybe he disapproves of Clarabell's seltzer squirting, or of something that mean old Phineas T. Bluster has just said. No matter. Howdy is smiling, but he is not happy.

This is the October that Dad buys me a clown costume for Halloween, a bright yellow-and-red, billowing affair with a rubber mask that is always smiling. When I put the mask on, Dad bursts out laughing at the sight of his five-year-old son who suddenly looks like a circus performer on drugs. "Are you smiling underneath that smiling mask?" he asks.

Of course I am, but what if I wasn't? Who would know?

On weekends, Peggy and I visit Mr. Bills. "You help me make cider, and I'll tickle you," he promises. The cider-making machine in his barn is a steel vat taller than Mr. Bills, with a canvas conveyor belt that takes apples up to the top opening and dumps them into the unseen mechanism that squashes the juice from them. Mr. Bills climbs a stepladder to look down into it, then climbs down and turns a tap to pour himself a glass of fresh apple juice. "Potentially potent," he says. We like the sound of the phrase, but we wonder what it means.

"There's a whole tub of apples," he tells us. "Just put the good ones on the belt. No rotten apples, hear?"

I try to obey, but there are so many bad ones that I can't keep up with Peggy, who is lining up every apple she sees, making patterns on the belt, wavy processions of yellow and green and almost-red apples marching to their doom, while I find three or four per minute. "How do you find good ones?" I ask.

"I don't," she whispers, and we both giggle. "Everything goes!"

"Come on, speed it up!" Mr. Bills says. "What are you laughing at? I'll give you something to laugh at later!"

I reach into the washtub and grab apple after apple and place them on the belt. My thumb plops through oozing bruises where worms wiggle, but I put them on the belt anyway. Yellowjackets are buzzing around us, sliding back and forth in the air. Some of them land on the apples and go into the vat to die. Mr. Bills pulls the tap and takes another test sip. "Ah! Perfect!" he says.

When the tub is empty, he shuts the machinery down. The silence rings. Mr. Bills blows his nose into a huge red handkerchief and snaps the residue off into a corner of the barn. Then he grins with a mouthful of multicolored teeth. "Ready for the tickling game?" he asks.

"OK," Peggy says. "But no tummies. Just under my neck and under my arms."

"We'll see. Come on into my study."

He leads us into his tarpaper house, past the vat of spring water, and into the corner room that faces our house to the north and the never-ending building project to the west. He pulls down the torn green window shade on the north window, but not the one on the west window. On the east wall is a heavy oak door with a shiny brass knob and keyhole. A hook-and-eye lock sits below a chain lock. Below that is a freshly cut two-by-four supported by brackets on either side of the door.

"What's in there?" I ask.

"No one goes in there," he says. "Rats in there. Rats. You want to go where there's rats?"

"Uh-uh," I say. But of course I want to.

Mr. Bills sits in a big rocking chair in the middle of the room and pulls Peggy onto his lap. "Ticka-ticka-ticka!" he says, splattering stubby fingertips under Peggy's chin while she squeals in laughter. "Ticka-ticka-ticka!" he says, tickling under her arms. "Ticka-ticka-ticka!" he says, pawing down her legs. Then he stops and looks at me.

"Get behind me and wait, I'll do you next," he says. "And don't try going through that door. I've got eyes in back of my head."

"Where?" I say, climbing onto the back of his chair and almost pulling it over. I spread his thinning gray hair apart in the back of his head. "I don't see any eyes!" I say.

"Well, they're there, and I can see you. So just stand back and wait."

Then I hear a loud squeal from Peggy, uncontrollable laughter and the words, "No tummies! I said no tummies, heeheehee!"

I sneak a peek. Mr. Bills has Peggy's jersey half off and is furiously tickling her tummy, a bead of sweat on his forehead, his cheeks getting red, while Peggy laughs and wishes she could cry.

10

The earache makes me writhe on the living room davenport in agony, while Mom tries all her nursing tricks to make the pain go away. St. Joseph Aspirin doesn't touch it. She doesn't have time to make chicken soup, and a can of Campbell's Chicken and Noodle is too watery. I can barely pry my jaws apart anyway. Dad opens his hearing aid bag, wipes his otoscope with alcohol-soaked cotton, proud that he has this expensive medical instrument even though he's not a doctor. He pulls my earlobe down as gently as he can, and I scream in pain. His hands are icy, and so is the metal otoscope.

"Red as a beet," he says. "Better call Dr. Markwald."

Heinz Markwald reminds me of Groucho Marx from "You Bet Your Life," the quiz show we watch on the Nickersons' Sylvania. The doctor has a black mustache and black eyebrows, wears black-rimmed eyeglasses, and talks fast and funny. He carries a black bag that looks like Dad's, pulls out an otoscope just like Dad's, turns on the otoscope's light and aims the beam at me like a ray gun from a space movie.

"So, again you're sick? Now what? When are you going to kick the bucket, so I can get some sleep?"

"Kick what?"

"Never mind. What for you are sick?"

"I ... I don't know."

"You don't know, you don't know. You make me get out of bed at one in the morning, least you could do is know why you got sick. What now, broken leg?"

"No."

"Appendicitis?"

"What?"

"Never mind. What's the matter with you?"

"My ear hurts."

"That's all? We should cut it off?"

"No!" I shout, then wince in pain.

"Aha. Hurts when you say no, eh? Don't talk so loud."

Then he smiles, and his voice gets smoother.

"OK, little guy, let's see what you got in there. John, turn the room lights off, will you?"

"Uh, sure, Doctor. Why?"

"Why? Because I can see better in the dark, John. Try it with your hearing aid customers."

The room goes dark except for the otoscope's pinhole light, bright with its concentrated beam. He pulls my earlobe gently, and it doesn't hurt. The otoscope isn't cold, but he's a little rougher than Dad was, peering all up and down the ear canal, describing what he sees.

"You grow potatoes in here, Jack?"

"No."

"Don't lie. There's a carrot in here too. No wonder it hurts. But at least you won't go hungry."

Mom is laughing in the dark, and Dad is chuckling too. Dr. Markwald is putting on a show for them. I don't know if he's kidding or not. After all, Dad said he saw a red beet in my ear.

"Penicillin," the doctor says, wiping his otoscope as the lights come back on. "A needle in the rear, for the ear. Lie on your stomach."

I'm afraid of the needle, but I turn over, waiting for the stab. With my face in the sofa cushion, I hear him rummage for his syringe.

"All right, now just hold still and—what's this?" he says.

I turn to look up at his mock-angry face. "What?" I say.

"You're bashful? How can you get a needle if you don't show your gluteus maximus?"

He pulls my bottoms down and says, "There, did that hurt?"

Now I'm relieved. I didn't feel a thing. "No," I say.

A quick sharp pain in my butt, then the feel of cool alcohol, and he pulls my bottoms back up. "That's the one and only time I can try that trick with you," he says. "As long as the pain's gotta come, might as well get it when you don't expect it. Then it's not so bad."

"Will you bill me, Doctor?" Dad says as Markwald is drawing on his long black coat.

"Bill you? Waste of time."

"Well then, can I pay a little at a—"

"John! It's one-thirty in the morning. I don't charge for house calls between midnight and dawn on alternate Thursdays."

"It's Friday morning," Dad says.

Dr. Markwald glares at him, then smiles. "Don't push it, John. Good night," he says.

The door closes behind him. Dad stares out the window for a few seconds, then breaks the silence. "Did you hear what he said, Marion?"

"Yes. That was kind of him."

"You can see better in the dark," Dad says. "I never would have thought of it."

11

The woman standing on the edge of a grassy, rocky driveway is spooning something yellow and pulpy into my mouth. She is laughing at my puffed cheeks and my tears, heedless of my unwillingness to swallow whatever this is she is scooping from a brown mixing bowl. "One more bite, that's it, open up," Aunt Jane says. It is impossible to open my mouth without losing the glop that's inside it, so I force myself to swallow some. There is absolutely no taste to it, which is worse than a bad taste, because there is no way to identify it for future reference. It isn't too salty, or too sweet, or too sour, or too bitter. It isn't even too hot or too cold. It isn't too hard to chew, because it's thick and soupy. I never do find out what it is.

Except for this first glimpse of her, Aunt Jane is not the ogre of everyone's childhood. She is not grumpy or gout-ridden. She doesn't complain of ailments ending in -itis or speak of operations ending in -ectomy. She doesn't wear long black dresses or carry an umbrella when it's sunny. She doesn't ride a broomstick, and her cats are not black. Aunt Jane is short and thin, spry, bright-eyed, and always either talking or laughing. And her mysterious food is not a punishment; she believes it is an act of pure love.

On this sweaty Fourth of July in 1952, she is throwing a picnic at her upstate New York farm and has invited the seven Sheedys to join the nine Nesbitts. Aunt Jane's eight kids—she calls them the Eight Snuffs, for reasons that are not clear until years later—range in age from fifteen to three. Mom's five kids range from seven-year-old Peggy to twenty-three-month-old Gerald. Mom walks by carrying him in her arms, and Aunt Jane clinks the spoon and bowl onto a picnic table, and goes, "Ooh, look at the little guy with the big blue eyes! Just like—" She hesitates, as if trying to remember a name. "Well, just like his grandmother!"

Mom laughs. "Oh, no, Mother had hazel eyes, Jane."

"Are you sure? Oh, what do I know! I was only twelve when she died."

"Well, you should remember, then," Mom says. "I was only six, but I remember her eyes were hazel."

Jane tickles Gerald under the chin and says, "Well, no matter, he's just the cutest little button there ever was!"

My grandmother, blue- or hazel-eyed Alice, died on March 26, 1918, a few days after giving birth to her twelfth child, my Uncle John. Mom was sent to live with her father's sister, Mary, and her husband, Moses Doyle, in Torrington. Uncle John, the infant, went into an orphanage for a time, then to his grandmother in Torrington. Three siblings—Tom, Jane and Louise—stayed with their father, Alexander McElhone, a factory mechanic who chased jobs from Ridgefield to Bridgeport, Connecticut. Other siblings were divided among other relatives.

When Mom gets together with her sisters or brothers, it is not the same as when Dad drives us to Danvers, Massachusetts, to visit our Sheedy relatives. When we visit that homestead, the Sheedy uncles and aunts sit in overstuffed chairs and read *The Boston Globe* without uttering a word for hours. Maybe Uncle Bob will finally say, "Says heah the tide is high at one-oh-faw this afternoon." And his sister, my Aunt Margaret, will say, "Well well well." Then an hour of silence, except for the tocking and chiming of seven grandfather clocks. Finally, Aunt Eleanor will say, "Well, it's a hot one, but we've got good air." And Uncle Bob will rattle the full-color Dick Tracy page and say, "Mmm-hmm."

But Mom's relatives never stop talking. They must socialize with all their might. The McElhone Diaspora created in the separated siblings a longing to get back together, to reclaim something denied them by their mother's sudden death.

Aunt Jane cannot drink in enough of my brother Gerald. She cannot take her own bright blue gaze away from him.

On our visit to Danvers a few weeks earlier, Dad's sister Margaret simply clucked, "Well well well, what a fine young boy. More tea, Marion?" And Mom simply said, "No thank you," without reminding Aunt Margaret that she drank coffee, never tea.

I am glad that Aunt Jane is ignoring me now, because I don't have to eat any more yellow stuff. I wish I could spit out what I have, but if I do I'll be scolded by her husband. Right now, Uncle Jim is yelling at seven-year-old Ben, the younger of their two boys. "You pick that watermelon seed up right now! Who taught you to spit watermelon seeds all over the lawn?" he booms.

There really is no lawn on the farm. There is grass. Tall grass by the fire pond, short grass by the driveway, dandelions gone to seed, wild strawberry plants scrambling among scrubby patches of weeds and rocks. But the soil for the vegetable garden is rich with manure from a half dozen Holsteins, two of which are nursing calves sired by the two big bulls in a lower pasture. Three rows of shin-high corn are flanked by long rows of pole beans, tomatoes, prickly little cucumbers, yellow squash, leaf lettuce, and cabbage.

"Pick up all those seeds, damn you!" Uncle Jim is shouting, and Ben is muttering something while he pretends to find black watermelon seeds in the black dirt.

"How did you find your way up here?" Mom is asking Aunt Jane.

"The Albany Turnpike," Aunt Jane says.

"I mean, you lived in Paterson, a big city. Now you're out in nowhere."

"Well, remember, Marion, we went to New Jersey so Father could find better work," Aunt Jane says. "Work dried up in Bridgeport, so he took us on the road. He went to South Boston in the early Twenties, taking Tom and me and little Louise. Tom and I were getting to be teenagers, but Louise was only about seven when we went to Boston. When we moved again to Paterson, she was ten. Tom found work there right away, but I had to stay home. Father worked, Tom worked, and I stayed home to keep house and raise little Louise."

"You must have had a dreary existence," Mom says.

"Oh, there were … there were diversions," Aunt Jane says with a nervous giggle that almost ends in a sob. "And eventually, Louise grew old enough to work at a telephone switchboard for a large company, so my life got easier. And then I met Jim. He had this farmland from his family, so we moved here."

"But there's nobody up here. It's like you and Jim are trying to get away or something."

"Get away? Look at these kids. I love kids, but you can't get away from them," Aunt Jane says. "And I would never want to."

I walk slowly away from Mom and Aunt Jane and watch Peggy pretending to help Ben find watermelon seeds. Uncle Jim has ambled away, a lanky, suspendered man in a tee shirt. Suddenly Peggy says, "I found one!" and pops a watermelon seed into her mouth.

"Don't eat that!" Ben says. "My mother says if a girl eats a watermelon seed, she'll have a baby!"

Peggy spits out the seed. Blue-eyed Gerald begins to cry.

A sudden Catskill thunderstorm chases everyone inside the massive stone house, where the beer and highballs flow freely among the grown-ups. Mom and Aunt Jane playfully dance the can-can to a scratchy 78-rpm recording of Offenbach. Dad entertains with Harry Lauder ballads, with a wonderful Scottish burr perfected from listening intently to his own record collection. Dad proudly announces his acrobatic daughter Peggy, who astounds the grown-ups with her backbends and splits. I receive polite applause for balancing a broom handle on my finger.

In the evening, the storm clears in time for Uncle Jim's fireworks. Sparkling rockets shoot over the barn's roof, and pinwheels spin out every color there is. Mom, Dad, and twelve kids gaze unblinking at the display.

But the youngest and the oldest of the group are not paying attention. Gerald is fast asleep, and Aunt Jane is holding him in her arms, looking down at him with a shine in her eyes.

12

Except for the one bright spot, the visit to Aunt Jane, there is a cloud hanging over my summer of 1952. I have to start first grade in September, and I don't want to go.

In a ragged flurry of memory, I see my six-year-old self fighting with my first button-down-the-front shirt, hearing Mom raging at me to "Make it snappy" or "Shake a leg." Snaps would be easier than buttons, I remember thinking, but shaking my leg couldn't possibly help me line up each button with its corresponding buttonhole. "Get a move on," she says, licking her hand and smoothing my cowlick. "Come on, hop to it."

I am a half hour late for my very first day at Saint Mary's Parochial School in New Hartford. Laces dangling from my Buster Brown shoes, I hustle up the eight wide cement steps of the Victorian Gothic schoolhouse as fast as my short legs will allow, my right hand in Mom's grip. The walnut-stained wainscoting is taller than I am, and I catch the scent of varnish on freshly sanded floors. Our footsteps echo down the dim, narrow corridor, past a plaster statue of the barefooted Blessed Mother standing on a snake, and stop before a tall brown door with a windowed transom too high for even the tallest grown-up to see through.

If I am unused to squeaky-tight shoes and starched shirts, nothing could have prepared me for the sight on the other side of that door. At my mother's knock, the door swings open to reveal a tall, slender woman in the blackest dress I have ever seen. It starts with a black, flowing shawl and goes all the way down to her black shoes. Under her chin is a white half circle as big as a sofa cushion. Dozens of rattling, black, pecan-size beads are gathered on a string by her side.

"Good morning, Mrs. Sheedy," the woman says. She smiles, then glances down at me quickly with her eyes only, keeping her head level. "Is this John?"

She is referring to me, but it takes me a minute to realize it. My baptismal name is John, the same as my father and his father, the same as Mom's brother and great-grandfather, the same as my cousin and a bunch of other relatives. Dad insisted on naming me John, and Mom agreed as long as I was called Jack, to avoid confusion.

"Yes, Sister Mary Richard," Mom says. "I'm sorry he is late. We had trouble dressing this morning."

I have no memory of the rest of that day. If I am not the only one crying, I am not aware of that fact. If none of the other kids is watching me blubbering my eyes out, I imagine they all are. If Sister Mary Richard thinks she is entertaining us with picture book stories, turning the open book outward to show us what Brer Rabbit looks like, I only think she is inflicting on us the pain of learning. Somehow, I know these are not stories; these are lessons, and I hate them. I hate knowing that I will be in this old four-classroom building for eight years, then in some bigger building for four years, and maybe in another, even bigger building, for four more years—"if you apply yourself," Dad keeps saying.

First and second grades are in the same classroom. Across the hall, where the barefoot Virgin Mary is crushing the snake, grades three and four share a room. Upstairs is the same arrangement: grades five and six are in the room above us, and grades seven and eight are in the room across from that.

Peggy is in the third grade, across the hall from me. She is less than a year older than I, but, as Mom vaguely explains, because she was born after March 31, she is two grades ahead of me. I am baffled by the math. If I were five weeks younger, would I have started school a year sooner? Or was I simply kept out of school for a year just so I would never be in the same classroom as Peggy?

After school, Peggy and I grab hands and run across the strawberry patch to visit Mr. Bills. He is walking around the skeleton of the house he is building, looking for protruding nail heads that need banging. "Daddy says you're never gonna finish building the house," Peggy says, even though Dad has told her not to tell him he said so.

"He did, did he? Well, maybe he's right. It's my life's work, you know. When it's done, maybe I'm done too."

"Done with what?" Peggy says.

"Done with livin. Never mind," he says. "It's almost apple cider time. You gonna help me again this year?"

"I guess," Peggy says without enthusiasm.

Mr. Bills laughs, and the laugh turns to coughing, and he can't seem to stop. He covers his coughing with a dirty gray handkerchief, then looks at it and whispers, "Jesus!" Peggy and I bow our heads, because that's what the Sisters of Saint Joseph have told us to do when we hear that name. "Jesus Christ, there's blood," Mr. Bills mutters. "You kids go on home now."

The skeleton house sits unfinished for yet another winter, while Mr. Bills is in the hospital, then in some other place. "Mom says he went to a place to dry off," Peggy tells me.

"How did he get wet?" I ask.

"How should I know!"

"Well, how come you have to go to a hospital when you get wet?"

"How do I know? And it's not a hospital, it's a Sigh Land. Ask Mom."

When it's time for my bath that night, I tell Mom I don't want to have to go to a Sigh Land to dry off. "What on earth are you talking about?" she sputters.

"Like Mr. Bills."

She squints, then says, "Oh. Well, Mr. Bills isn't drying off. He's drying out. In an *asylum*. He drinks, you know."

This still isn't clear. I'm OK with giving up bathing, but do I have to quit Kool-Aid as well?

Mom never baked more apple pies than she did in 1952. Bertha Atkins, Mr. Bills's live-in companion, is not strong enough to make cider, and she ends up giving away most of the apples that year. Peggy and I are still free to wander around Mr. Bills's property, and one day we wander into the tickling room, where the shades are drawn and the room is in green shadow. The empty tickling chair sits in the middle of the room, and we avoid it. Behind it is the door, still barricaded with a two-by-four, where Mr. Bills told us rats lived. We peer through the keyhole.

Peggy says, "I don't see anything."

I push on the two-by-four, and it lifts up from its metal brackets. Peggy helps me to lean it against a wall, and we open the door to the forbidden room.

It's just a closet with shelves on the back wall, floor to ceiling, stacked with dozens of dust-coated gallon jugs of cider. Red cardboard tags are tied to strings that are knotted around the jugs' finger loops. The tags record the cider vintage, beginning around 1945 and continuing to 1951. There are some spiders, but no rats.

We walk outside and gaze at the skeleton house. "I bet he never finishes it," she says.

"Why not?"

"Cuz then he'll die. That's what he said."

"Mom says everybody dies. So what difference does it make?"

"If he finishes it, he dies right then. If he doesn't finish it, he dies later."

I imagine two things. Mr. Bills comes home feeling fine, gets truckloads of lumber and shingles and clapboards and bricks and cement mix and finishes the house. As he bangs the last nail in the roof, he clutches his chest and rolls down the asphalt shingles and lands with a thud in the strawberry patch.

The second thing I imagine is Mr. Bills coming home feeling fine, looking at the unfinished skeleton house and saying, "That's it, I quit, I'll never pound another nail." And in my fantasy, the skeleton house grows old and leans and finally topples over. Peggy and I are old people with canes, watching the weathered boards creaking and toppling, while we stand next to Mr. Bills, who hasn't aged a whisker in eighty years. "It couldn't stand forever, and it couldn't ever be finished," I imagine him saying. "But at least I was safe while it stood."

Then Mr. Bills, one hundred and thirty-nine years old, clutches his chest and falls dead in the strawberry patch.

13

Dad either has no money or a fistful. When he makes a hearing aid sale, he spends the whole profit. He also spends the cost. In April 1953, he splurges on an outdoor swing set, which he installs himself by inserting the steel legs into buckets of wet cement that he has placed in four holes in the back lawn. When the cement dries, he fills in the holes with dirt.

I hear Peggy's screams just as I am flushing the toilet. I look out the bathroom window, but the barn is in the way. I hear Mom's footsteps racing through the house, then the sound of the sun porch door slamming. Peggy's screams go on and on, and before I can get out of the bathroom, Mom and Peggy are in the 1941 Chrysler Dad just bought on credit and are heading up to the emergency room in Winsted.

Peggy is still whimpering when she comes home, her right arm in a cast. She says she tried jumping off the swing but got tangled in the chain and landed wrong. She broke her arm.

While she is upstairs crying herself to sleep, I climb the swing set and peer into the crossbar where wasps are building a nest. The wasps do not appreciate my curiosity. About six of them attack my right eyelid, and I scream. Mom pulls me down and yells at me, then puts baking soda on my eyelid and sends me to the bedroom I still share with Peggy.

A few days later, the new RCA Victor television arrives, paid for with the promise of a hearing aid sale that eventually falls through. Peggy and I sit and groan in pain together. "Just like last year, remember?" Peggy says.

"What?"

"When we had our tonsils out. You know, we were in the same hospital room and everything. First they took me, then they took you."

"Oh, yeah. I hope we never get a sore throat like that again."

"I couldn't even eat my soup."

"They said they'd bring ice cream, but they never did," I say.

"The hospital was so boring," Peggy says, twisting the channel knob just in time to hear Buffalo Bob say, "Say kids, what time is it?"

At least now we have Clarabell to cheer us up.

Two binaural hearing aid sales in May prompt Dad to finally do something to keep us from running out of water, and he hires a contractor to drill an artesian well. Peggy and I are with Mom at the Schlossers' house down the road, when the Schlossers' phone rings three times. "That's us," Mr. Schlosser says. His face turns white. "Marion, go home, your house is on fire!"

"Stay here!" Mom orders me. My right eye is still swollen shut, but through my left eye I see the blaze on the drilling rig as Mom and Peggy run toward it on the shoulder of Route 44. Even though it must hurt her arm, Peggy is running. Mr. Schlosser hobbles quickly out of the house. "I called the Pine Meadow Fire Department," he says. "They're just a half mile away, they'll be here in a minute." Then he takes my hand and walks me to my house.

The house was never on fire, but the drilling rig was, from a spark that ignited some oil-soaked rags in the truck. The men put the blaze out quickly with fire extinguishers. Thirty minutes later the Pine Meadow fire truck rolls slowly into our driveway, no siren, no flashing lights. "Sorry we're late, ma'am," the driver says with an embarrassed chuckle. He is still sitting in the cab, his left arm draped out the window and a Chesterfield dangling from his fingers. "We couldn't get the truck started. Where's the fire?"

In June, Dad drives Peggy and me to Worcester, Massachusetts, to see the damage caused by a rare tornado that hit that city. "It could happen anywhere," Dad tells us. "It isn't very common in this part of the country. Usually they get tornadoes down South."

"Or in Kansas," Peggy says.

"That's right," Dad says.

"Like in the *Wizard of Oz*, right? When Dorothy and Toto got blown away and found the Tin Man and the Straw Man and the Lion, and they all got on the yellow brick road and went to Oz."

"I hate that movie," I say.

"How come?" Peggy says, trying to scratch under her cast.

"Because they're all looking for the Wizard of Oz, but there really isn't any such person. Some pretender made it all up, and he lied. It's just a dumb movie."

Dad says, "Didn't you like that story, Jack? I thought you and Peggy loved it when we took you to see it."

"Yeah, until the end."

"But at the end, everybody got what they were looking for, didn't they?"

"They were looking for the Wizard. And he was a fake."

"No, he wasn't. He was real," Dad says. "He didn't need to be a Wizard. He knew what everybody wanted, and he showed all of them that they already had it."

"Yeah," Peggy says. "Don't you get it?"

Worcester's damaged area is barricaded by police cars to protect against looting, and so we don't really see much. We have come all this way, and then we have to turn around and go home. Dad and Peggy think we have had a great ride, but I don't. I want to see houses blown to smithereens, telephone poles knocked down, electrical wires sparking, homes on fire, explosions—anything indicating some kind of disaster. But there is nothing. Just a couple of black Ford police cruisers at an intersection, and not even a crowd of people lining up to see anything. We drive all the way to Worcester and never see anything, just like Dorothy never saw the Wizard of Oz. And we turn around and just come home. I don't like this kind of ending at all.

14

I am playing with one of those wooden birdcalls. You twist one lipstick tube-sized cylinder against another one nestled inside it and it chirps like a Baltimore oriole, or a robin, or a barn swallow. I climb the splintery ladder of the hayloft this morning and twist the birdcall. I don't know which bird I am imitating, but the barn swallows must know it is a species that threatens their just-hatched young in their nest in the rafters. Both parents swoop into the wide window and buzz me, letting me know I am where I should not be.

"Where'd you GO?"

It is Peggy, calling me from the driveway near the strawberry patch. I don't answer.

"JACK!"

I twist the birdcall once in reply. The swallows flutter outside the window but do not buzz me. They are catching on.

"Where *ARE* you?"

I twist the birdcall in imitation of Peggy's short-long-short three syllables.

Tuh-*WEEE*-it!

"*Ja*-ack!"

Twee-it!

"Where did you *GO*?"

Tuh-wee-wee-*WEEET*!

No way does this last call sound like a bird. Peggy pauses, then shouts, "Where *ARRR-RRRE* yooooo-ou?"

I know this is a trick but I fall for it. Challenged by the long syllables, I twist the cylinder first quickly, then as slowly as I can to extend the second syllable. It's too slow, and no sound comes out. It doesn't matter. Peggy has homed in on the direction of the first syllable and is running through the open garage and into the adjoining stable below the hayloft.

"I see you! How come you didn't answer?"

"There's baby birds up here," I say.

"I know *THAT!*" she says, pulling herself through the scuttle with her good left arm.

Peggy always knows everything. She knew that Mr. Bills's baby chicks had hatched even before I told her last week. I had been helping Bertha feed the chickens, since Mr. Bills was still in the Sigh Land, and Bertha had said, "Want to see something no one's seen yet?" She flung open the door to the henhouse, and the floor was carpeted in yellow, chirping fuzz. I ran home to tell Peggy, who said, "I know *THAT!*" A few minutes later, she put her Nancy and Sluggo comic book down and said, as nonchalantly as she could manage, "Let's go see the baby chicks again."

Now, in the hayloft, she says, "Anyway, I'd rather play records than watch baby birds. So quit playing with that birdcall or you'll get all the birds in Puddletown in here."

Peggy has made her entrance and now dominates the stage. In her presence, I am a bit player. She struts across the wide, creaking floorboards, ducking to avoid the sloping roofline, and stops at the walnut-veneered Edison phonograph in the very center of the loft. Her right arm is still in the cast, but without the sling. With her left arm, she opens the hinged lid and examines the 78-rpm hill-and-dale disc on the turntable. "This is a good one," she says, and she tries to wind the crank handle on the side of the phonograph. "You do it," she commands, rubbing her cast. I wind it up and place the heavy stylus arm on the disc. Peggy releases the brake. The scratchy voice of Irish tenor John McCormack floats from the cone-shaped speaker:

> *Thou wouldst still be adored as this moment thou art,*
> *Let thy loveliness fade as it will ...*

We listen in silence to "Believe Me If All Those Endearing Young Charms," awed by the singer's range, and Peggy takes my hand. When the song is over, she rummages among the other ancient recordings. "We'll play this one now," she decides, placing another disc by McCormack on the turntable.

Oh Danny Boy, the pipes, the pipes are ca-allin'
From glen to glen an' down the mountainside ...

Again, Peggy takes my hand, and we listen in silence. McCormack has a beautiful, high voice, and when he sings the phrase "but take me *ba-ack*, when summer's in the me-eadow," I can't believe any man can really sing so high. But when he sings, "It's I'll be *he-eere* in sunshine or in shadow," I almost want to cry, and so does Peggy. She squeezes my hand but doesn't say a word.

Peggy plays this record over and over again, and her lips start to move along with the lyrics. At the fifth playing, she is singing along, seemingly unaware anymore of my presence.

That night, Dad has a few Miller High Lifes and entertains the family with his favorite Harry Lauder ballads. Peggy says, "It's my turn! I want to sing 'Danny Boy.'"

Dad looks at his pride and joy, his firstborn child. "Well, yes, why not?" he says. "Ladies and gentlemen, next on the Ted Mack Amateur Hour is Peggy Sheedy, and here she is!"

Peggy jumps up and stands in the center of the living room, while the rest of the family is gathered on the davenport. She pulls the wooden birdcall from her pocket and chirps it once. Then she pulls me by the hand and gets me to stand next to her. She chirps the birdcall while she sings, looking right at me:

Oh Jacky boy, the pipes, the pipes are ca-alling,
From glen to glen and down the mountainside,
The summer's gone and all the leaves are fa-alling,
Oh Jacky boy, oh Jacky boy, I love you so.

15

George Hough is cuckoo again. He stumbles across the garden carrying an M1917 American Enfield rifle. Dad spots him and tells Peggy and me to get in the house. From the living room, I listen at the window.

"Ish OK, John," George slurs. "Ish not loaded. Wash this."

"Put it down, George," Dad says.

"Ev'thin's fine, jush wash."

Dad spots me looking out the window. "Jack, put your head down! George, give me that gun."

"Wanna show you how you shoot thish."

"George, ooh! George!" It's Minnie's sour, nasal whine. I don't see her. My head is down, and I'm looking into Peggy's terrified hazel eyes.

"It's all right, Minnie," Dad's voice soothes. "George, that's a fine-looking gun. Could I see it now?"

"Don't try takin' my rifle, John. Ish my infantry rifle, from nineteen-seventeen. Wash thish."

"Ooh, John, do something!"

I stand up to look out the window. Dad is pointing over George's shoulder. Peggy pulls my arm from below. "Get down, Jack!" she whispers.

"No, I want to look."

"George, what's over there?" Dad says.

"Don't trick me, John," But George looks over his shoulder anyway, and Dad lunges for the rifle, grabbing it in a quick motion.

"Ooh!" Minnie says.

"What—?" George says.

"It's all right, George," Dad says.

"What are they doing?" Peggy asks me.

"Dad's got the gun."

"Ooh!" Minnie whines again.

"Aw, John, you tricked me, didn't you?" George is almost whimpering. "Ish not loaded, you know. Ish ver' shafe."

"Come inside," Dad says. "Maybe you could have some coffee."

"Miller High Life French Roasht?" George says, then chuckles over his joke. "Lesh go inside, John."

I duck down. Dad enters first, carrying the rifle, barrel pointed toward the floor. Minnie follows, supporting a teetering George. "Sit here," Dad tells George. "Peggy, where's your mother?"

"She's coming. She's getting blueberries. Bertha's got blueberries for us."

"Minnie, can you make coffee?" Dad says. "You know our kitchen."

"Hee hee, all right. George, you be good."

Peggy is staring out the window, her back to everyone. George is trying not to get sleepy as he sits in the big, soft, brown, easy chair. "George, look, you were frightening my children," Dad says.

"Aw, John, I didn't mean nothin'. Right, Jacky?"

Minnie comes in with a steaming cup in a saucer. "That was quick," Dad says.

"You had a pot left from breakfast. I heated it on the Glenwood," Minnie says. "Here's a bag of doughnuts from Bertha's, too. Is it all right to give him one? His sugar gets low."

"Yes, of course," Dad says.

George sips the coffee and bites into Bertha's greasy old-fashioned doughnut. A large brown crumb rolls off his pant leg and onto the carpet. Minnie crumples the empty doughnut bag and puts it in the wastebasket.

Peggy is still gazing out the window. Everyone is quiet for a minute. I take the crumpled paper bag from the wastebasket and walk over to George. "George, you see this bag?" I say.

"Cat's in the bag," George says.

"No, you are!" I say.

There is a half second of silence, then Dad and Minnie burst out laughing at the same time. George begins laughing after five or six seconds, then looks puzzled. Peggy does not turn around.

I hear the kitchen screen door slam shut. "John, are you here?" Mom's voice lilts.

"We're in the living room," Dad says. "The Houghs are here."

"Oh, good! Look what I have!" Mom says, bursting into the living room carrying a stainless steel colander overflowing with marble-sized blueberries. Peggy has turned around at the sound of Mom's voice and now runs toward her and hugs her leg, causing half the blueberries to scatter along the carpet and down George's low-slung white undershirt. There are tears in Peggy's eyes.

"Peggy, you're spilling my berries!" Mom says. "What's wrong?"

"He had a gun!" Peggy says.

"Who? Had what?"

"It's all right now," Dad says.

"Ooh, dear!" Minnie whimpers.

"We can wash those berries off, I guess," Mom says, absently looking at the blue constellations on the light beige carpet. "Don't step on them. Oh! Wait! I almost forgot."

Mom pulls away from Peggy's grip and disappears into the kitchen with the colander. She returns in three seconds holding the hand of an old, weak, very thin man who wears a faded red plaid shirt half-tucked into blue dungarees.

"Look who's here!" she says to everyone.

No one registers any recognition.

"Well? Can't you at least welcome him back after a whole year?"

"Who is it, Mom?" I finally ask.

"You don't recognize him?" Mom says.

"Um, no," I say.

"It's Mr. Bills!"

The gaunt old man smiles wanly and lifts a shaky hand to wave.

Dad's mouth drops open. His hand tightens on the trigger of George's rifle. He blows a deafening hole in the floor, right through to the basement, shattering a Mason jar filled with piccalilli that Mom canned in 1949.

Minnie collapses in a faint. "I'm ... it's good," Mr. Bills mumbles. "It's good to be ..." But Mr. Bills stands ignored in a corner as Mom rubs Minnie's wrist and Dad fans her with a *Life* magazine.

16

"I may have told you this before," Dad said a few years before he died in 1997. "But it bears repeating. When you tell a story, even if it's true, there are rules. A gun over the fireplace in Act One must be fired in Act Two. Otherwise, there is no reason for the gun. And also, did I ever mention you have to embellish? I did? Well, it bears repeating."

George Hough's rifle, of course, never went off. It never even entered our house. Everything else in that episode happened, though not necessarily on the same day or in the same place. Cuckoo George did bring his World War I rifle into our yard, and Dad did talk him into handing it over. On another occasion, I did tell George he was in the bag. On another occasion, Mom brought blueberries home from Bertha. And on still another occasion, Mr. Bills, barely recognizable due to his weight loss, returned home. Does it really matter that they didn't all happen within five minutes?

Dad often entertained us with daydreams. That's what he called the impromptu stories he told us. "Tell us a daydream!" Peggy would demand.

"What about?" he would ask. We always had to supply the subject.

"About a mattress!" I would say, because we were in bed.

"Once upon a time, there were a little girl and a little boy who sailed down the river on a Sealy Posturepedic Mattress," he would begin. It was a Huck Finn kind of odyssey, and the details have vanished into time.

If Dad had been asked to tell a daydream about Peggy and me, it may have sounded like this:

Once upon a time, there was an eight-year-old boy name Jack, who had a nine-year-old sister Peggy and three younger siblings. His sister Ann sucked her thumb and talked to herself. His brother Tom talked baby talk until he was six years old and wore a patch over his eye to correct for something called amblyopia. Their father called the patch an occludah, *which Jack thought was a real word until he realized years later that it was his father's Boston accent dropping the r in* occluder. *Jack's brother Gerald imitated Tom's speech habits, but only, the speech therapist said, because he looked up to him— like Jack looked up to Peggy. Jack thought these younger siblings were strange and did not associate with them. But he followed Peggy everywhere.*

Peggy's dresses were kept in a metal wardrobe in the boys' bedroom, because Peggy's room was too small. One morning, Jack wanted to see what it felt like to be Peggy, so he pulled a long blue dress from the wardrobe and slipped it on. It felt cool and dry and slippery, but almost abrasive, not friendly like his cotton jerseys. And, of course, it was too long—it draped over his feet like the Statue of Liberty's green robes, or maybe like the statue of the Virgin Mary stepping on the snake in the halls of Saint Mary's School. Jack was reaching for a pair of red patent leather shoes in the bottom of the wardrobe when Peggy walked in, stopped, stared with wide hazel eyes, and turned and ran downstairs. Jack's face felt hot, and he pulled the dress off and carelessly hung it back up and then tried to listen at the top of the stairs. He heard fragments of his mother's whisperings, phrases like "normal curiosity" and "but if it happens again." Peggy clomped up the stairs, pulled the dress off the hanger and tossed it in the laundry hamper at the top of the stairs.

One day in the summer of 1954, Peggy and Jack went off to swimming lessons at Goose Green Beach in the Barkhamsted Reservoir. Peggy was in the advanced class, and Mr. Koscak, the Red Cross swimming instructor, was testing members of that class. "Swim out to the ropes and back," he told each one. Peggy swam all the way to the ropes and turned around and got halfway back when the wake of a passing boat swamped her. Mr. Koscak flung his clipboard across the beach, nearly hitting Jack with it, and dived into the water, pulling Peggy back with the classic hand-under-the-chin scissors stroke.

"*I was OK!*" *Peggy yelled at him as soon as they reached shore.*
"*I was treading water!*"

She would never admit to anyone that she had nearly drowned.

On another day, Peggy went to visit her friends, and young
Jack was left by himself. Did he play with his sister Ann? Oh no, Ann
talked to herself. Did he play with his brother Tom? Oh no, Jack could
not understand what Tom was saying. Did he play with his brother
Gerald? Oh no, Gerald was only four years old, half Jack's age. Jack
was very, very bored. He had many toys, but they were all boring too.
His dump trucks were stupid. Only one of them had a metal crank that
would tilt the cargo bed up. The others were like statues of trucks.
Even the wheels didn't turn. Jack had a Radio Flyer wagon, but that
was fun only when someone pulled him in it. He could put rocks in it
and pull the rocks around, but what for? The wagon had no radio, and
it couldn't fly, so why did they call it a Radio Flyer anyway?

He liked his Lionel electric train very much, because it actually
did what real trains do, but one day the locomotive's motor burned
out and the train was no good any more. He had a bicycle, but he
didn't know how to balance it. His father once tried to teach him,
but whenever his father let go of the bicycle, Jack fell. On this day,
when Peggy was away with her friends and Jack was bored with his
immobile toys, he walked into the sun porch and opened the door to
the garage and looked at his yellow Columbia bicycle leaning against
the wall. "I can ride that now," he said to himself. And he wheeled the
bicycle to the top of the driveway, straddled it, and pedaled it all the
way to the Lyn Gas Company across the railroad tracks. There was no
one to watch him do it, but that was all right with Jack.

When Peggy came back that afternoon, they climbed into the
hayloft and watched barn swallows feeding their young in the nest.
First the father bird came and gave the chirping babies a worm. Then
the mother delivered another worm. Finally, a third bird arrived, also
with a worm. "Who's that bird?" Jack asked his sister. "The neck
store neighbor?"

"No," Peggy said, unwrapping a Mars Bar and offering Jack a
bite. "Mom told me barn swallows have two bunches of baby birds
each year. The first bunch helps feed the second bunch."

"How come she told you that and didn't tell me?" Jack asked.

"She said I could tell you," Peggy said.

And Peggy and Jack chewed their Mars Bar and watched the
barn swallows. And, for the rest of that afternoon at least, they lived
happily ever after.

17

When Peggy is too busy to play with me, I can find plenty to do, thank you. The Sisters of Saint Joseph have taught me to read. I remember the day it happened. One day, Sister Mary Ernestine is reading to us from a Dick and Jane book, and the next minute she is showing us how the little black bits of the alphabet we recite actually can be shuffled around to form millions of combinations that symbolize every word we speak. Sister Ernestine points to the very first combination of alphabet letters that appears as a chapter title on the first page of the Dick and Jane book. The title of the chapter—and the first word I ever learn to recognize—is "Work."

It is not the word I would have chosen. I might have chosen "Play," but the authors, and perhaps the nuns too, may have thought that "Work" was appropriate—a hidden lesson, no doubt. During read-aloud sessions, I am called on to be the most active of participants, the Narrator. I am the one who says, "Dick said" or "Jane answered" every time Dick says something or Jane answers somebody. I am also the person who reads the paragraphs of description when no one in the story is talking. "Dick and Jane walked on the path. Spot came with them. Baby Sally wanted a bottle. They all went to see Mrs. Brown talking to Mr. Little. The day was sunny. Everybody was Catholic, including Spot. See Spot make the sign of the cross with his paws. Oh, oh, oh, look at that!"

In the year-and-a-half since learning to read, I put this skill to work by reading the *U.S. News & World Report* and *Newsweek* magazines that Dad stores in the hayloft. There is news about a war in Korea, which I think is pronounced "Cory," and there is a story about a World War II general who was elected President. His name is long and hard to pronounce, but his nickname is easy: Ike. There is a page in each issue of *Newsweek* called "Periscope"—a yellow page with double-spaced paragraphs that look like someone typed them on Dad's big Royal typewriter.

In the late summer of 1954, I find a book in the hayloft titled *Ripley's Believe It Or Not.* It is irresistible, because it combines pen-and-ink cartoons with hand-lettered copy. There are cartoon panels about African tribes with lips hanging down to their feet, Oriental women with fingernails that are ten feet long, and a story about a Mr. Coffee who had an automobile accident with a Mr. Pott, with the caption, "Grounds for a suit." I read this book by the hour, practically unaware that once again there is the sound of hammering and sawing from the Bills property across the strawberry patch.

When I climb down from the loft in the late August day, Mr. Bills is sitting on a straight-backed wooden chair near his skeleton house, mopping his gaunt face with a red handkerchief, and a half dozen men are covering the skeleton house with skin. No longer can I see Bertha's Tydol gas station through the bones of the house. Horizontal clapboards now cover it, and three men are just putting the last of the shingles on the roof. Mr. Bills's "life's work" will finally be completed.

Third grade begins. Sister Mary Josita is four feet tall. She has a red marking pencil and a wooden ruler. The pencil is for poking me on the top of my head when I am crying. The wooden ruler is for slapping my hand when the pencil poking doesn't make me stop crying. The crying is for something I cannot remember. I remember only the poking, the slapping, the crying, the horrible shame of crying in front of girls who see me every day.

In the winter, I get the measles. So does Peggy, and once again we are sick together, which is a comfort. I remember sleeping on the living room floor, away from Tom and Gerald upstairs in the boys' room, so they won't get sick. Ann has the measles too, and she sleeps on the living room floor along with Peggy and me.

The thirst is incredible. Mom and Dad have left glasses of juice for us to drink, but I have finished mine and want more. In the dark, with a pounding headache, too weak even to walk, I crawl on the floor toward the refrigerator and drain the last few drops of juice into my glass. It is still not enough, but even Mr. Bills's spring water never tasted this refreshing.

I am the last to recover and return to school. On my last day home, still sleeping in the living room alone, I get bored and take a volume of the maroon-covered *Standard Encyclopedia* down from the top of the upright piano. Either by accident or because I heard Dad or Mom talk about it, I find Abraham Lincoln's Gettysburg Address and read it. "Fourscore and seven years ago," it begins, "our fathers brought forth upon this continent a new nation, conceived in liberty and dedicated to the proposition that all men are created equal." I say the words out loud. I like the way they sound. I wonder if I could actually learn the whole speech by heart. That might be even more impressive than Peggy doing her acrobatics or singing "Danny Boy."

But how do you teach yourself a whole speech? And how do you know if you got it right? I read part of the first sentence again and then say it out loud, still looking at the text. Then I try it without looking at the text. I repeat the process until I know it's right. Then I tackle the rest of the sentence. After five minutes, I get the whole sentence memorized.

"Dad, listen," I say that night. "I know the Gettysburg Address."

"You what?"

"Oh, I'm sorry, I'll speak louder." I forget sometimes that Dad is hard of hearing, that he sells hearing aids because he wears one himself.

"No, I heard you," he says. "You just surprised me. You know the Gettysburg Address?"

"Fourscore and seven years ago our fathers brought—"

"Wow, that is really impressive. Marion, Jack just recited—"

"I'm not finished," I say. Dad underestimates his kids sometimes. Once, when Peggy was maybe two, he liked to make believe she was a prodigy. "Who first propounded the Theory of Relativity?" he would ask her in front of guests. "Einstein," was her cogent reply, as the guests politely cooed. But why make believe? Couldn't Peggy have learned to recite the sentence Dad framed as a question? Maybe even expounded on it? "Einstein was the first to propound the Theory of Relativity," she might have said. "He demonstrated that if the energy of a body changes by a given amount, then its mass must change by that given amount multiplied by the square of the speed of light." How many polite cooers would have failed to drop their jaws, their forks, and their notions of a child's limitations?

At other times, Dad would say to his assembled offspring, "All my kids are smart. Every one. You can do anything you want, be anything you want. You're all smart enough, if you apply yourselves." But I never could quite believe him. Dad was immensely smart, we all thought. A graduate of Boston College, class of 1935, liberal arts, read the classics in Greek and Latin. But he was a salesman. He was behind on the mortgage. He bought cars from the trade-in lot. Since I refused to believe myself equal to or greater than Dad in intelligence, how could I expect to outdo him?

A few years from now, Dad will buy me an Eveready lantern, and, because I like astronomy, he will take me outside at night and shine the beam at the constellations, telling me that even this slim beam of light can actually reach the stars. I will like this, because it doesn't sound like a lesson. I will like it even more when he shines the beam down at the flyleaf of a book on astronomy he is giving me, where he has drawn a picture of a wagon towing a star, followed by his penciled script: "Ah, mon fils! Hitch your wagon to a star!"

It all sounds so romantic. But how do you reach the stars when your father can barely reach the end of the month with his checkbook?

Mom comes into the living room, drying her hands on a dish towel. Peggy has a sudsy plate and dishrag in her hands. Ann walks in, sucking her thumb. Tom and Gerald bound in and start jumping on the sofa.

"Calm down, everyone!" Dad says. "Jack wants to show us something."

"—conceived in liberty and dedicated to the proposition that all men are created equal," I say.

The phone rings once, our ring. Mom goes into the den to answer it.

"Go ahead, Jack," Dad says. "The rest of us are listening."

"Oh, really?" Mom says into the phone in the next room. "Oh, I'm sorry."

"Kee goin!" Tom says to me.

I look at him. Tom spoke to me. "Keep going," he meant. Tom and I hardly ever speak. It's just Peggy and me, me and Peggy.

"Kee goin," Gerald says.

Ann pulls her thumb out of her mouth. "What's the rest?" she says.

I look at Peggy. Peggy is looking at Ann, Tom and Gerald. Now she looks at me and smiles. She just nods. Dad says, "Continue, Jack."

I recite the part about meeting on a great battlefield, but I'm listening with one ear to Mom talking on the phone.

"Well, we knew it was coming," Mom is saying.

"It is altogether fitting and proper that we should do this," I say.

"We will think of him often," Mom says. "We will remember him always for what he has done in the community."

"The world will little note, nor long remember—"

"—glad he hired those men to finish it," Mom is saying.

"… shall not perish from the earth," I finish up.

There is a stunned silence. Dad stares at me with a tear in his eye. Peggy continues to smile. Tom starts to clap, and then Gerald does, and Ann says, "Yay, Jack!"

Mom enters as the applause subsides, her mouth a straight line, her eyes colorless, her face like chalk.

"Mr. Bills died today," she says.

18

Late July, 1955. Already it is a long, hot summer, and it's not even half over. But on this sultry afternoon, as Mom and Dad and Peggy and I sit with Minnie and George on their screened-in back porch, we hear the rumble of distant thunder.

"Been a dry summer, John," George says, staring up at a darkening sky. It must be a weekday afternoon, because George, strictly a weekend drinker, is not cuckoo and does not have a can of Rheingold.

"Bad drought," Dad agrees. He is drinking a Cott ginger ale with ice. To set an example, or perhaps because Minnie quietly insisted, Dad is not drinking his Miller High Life and there is no liquor mixed with his ginger ale.

"My corn is only two feet high," Mom says. "The whole garden is drying out, and I'm still afraid to water it."

"Marion, that new artesian well will never run dry," Dad says.

"Starting to rain now," Minnie announces.

The drops are big and sudden, and they fall straight down. Within a minute it is a downpour, creating instant puddles that splash plump raindrops a foot high. Chunks of hail bounce off the roof of George's tool shed fifty feet away. We can only hear, not see this, because the tool shed is a watery blur of white clapboards through a thick curtain of rain. There is a bright flash of lightning, then instantly a crash of thunder, which rolls on forever.

"They're bowling again, kids," George says to Peggy and me. "The giants are bowling up in heaven."

We used to believe this. We don't any more, even though I want to. "Oh, right," I say. "Or maybe someone fell off a chair."

Two minutes later, the rain stops, as if God has abruptly put a plug in the clouds. The sun, behind us in the west, spotlights the hills across the Farmington River. The puddles are steaming.

"A lot of water," George says.

"But not enough," Minnie says. "Ground needs a good soaking. This won't do it."

"How much rain do we need?" I ask.

"Forty days and forty nights," Mom laughs, exhaling blue smoke from a Kool cigarette.

Peggy looks up at Mom. "Don't even joke like that, Mom," she says.

Minnie coughs nervously. No one says a word.

Early August, 1955. The dry heat wave continues. The clackety lawn mowers are silent for weeks at a time. The heat bugs drone on, still invisible, still never revealing to me how to avoid their sting, if indeed they do sting.

I am in the hayloft, reading Ripley's *Believe It Or Not*, when I hear Dad call, "Driving lesson!"

"Coming!" I shout. I clamber down the ladder with the book. I walk through the barn and into the garage, throw Ripley into the back seat of the '49 Chevy and climb into the driver's seat. Dad sits next to me.

"Depress the clutch," he instructs.

I extend my shoeless left foot, and the pedal goes only partway down before resisting.

"That's the brake," Dad says patiently. "Use the leftmost pedal."

This time I get it right, and the pedal goes all the way to the floor. I can barely see over the dashboard.

"Place the gear shift lever in neutral, just to be safe, and turn the key, while simultaneously pumping the accelerator," Dad says, as if reading from a textbook.

The car roars to life.

"Now, keep your left foot all the way down and ease the gear shift lever into reverse. That's it; now slowly depress the accelerator with your right foot while letting the clutch out gradually. Yes, one foot slowly comes up, the other slowly goes down. Watch your mirrors and back out of the garage carefully."

Miraculously, the car glides out of the garage and under the hanging willow branches. On Dad's command, I turn the wheel counterclockwise when we clear the garage, and the car curls around the low stone wall and into the access road to Lyn Gas. We start down the dirt drive to the crunch of pebbles and a cloying cloud of parched dust.

"Now we are going to attempt a maneuver," Dad says gently, trying not to sound alarmed as we approach a row of propane tanks near Lyn Gas. As though we have all the time in the world, he calmly says, "We are going to effect a cessation. Are you ready to try that?"

The Chevy isn't traveling very fast, but the row of propane tanks is looming larger in my view. I know what cessation means, but I don't say anything. Dad loves to use overqualified words in ordinary conversation.

"Now, what I want you to do is to rapidly release your right foot from the accelerator while simultaneously applying your left foot to the clutch and immediately your right foot to the brake. Also, to be safe, steer slightly to starboard." Dad's Boston accent makes the last word sound like "stabbid."

I am successful only in the last command, but it is sufficient, since it brings us to a cessation against a giant forsythia. The car and bush are unharmed, but the car has stalled.

"OK, you are going to have to perform a backup maneuver," Dad says. "Depress the clutch as you start the ignition. That's right, now, with the clutch down, move the gear shift control to the reverse position. Very good. Now observe your rear view mirrors. Can you see behind you?"

Of course I can't, and so Dad agrees to be my eyes and successfully guides me in the newly learned operation of backing up an automobile. "An important consideration to bear in mind," he adds as I approach the propane tanks again, "is never to back up an inch more than you have to."

The lesson is scarcely five minutes old, and yet I have had enough for one day. I pilot the Chevy up the driveway at a good ten miles an hour, then slow down expertly as I approach the turn toward the garage. As I guide the car toward the open garage, a low-hanging willow branch brushes against the windshield, momentarily distracting me.

"Apply the brake. Jack, the brake!"

The pedal goes all the way to the floor, because it is the clutch. The Chevy goes all the way through the left support of the garage opening, splintering wood and leaving a long, impressive scratch on the shiny black left front fender of Dad's car. Later that night, I hear him say to Mom that he thought of stepping on the brake himself, until he realized he would have crushed my bare foot.

Russell Rood, a handyman who lives in a trailer on Bertha's property, comes over a few days later and patches up the garage. Mr. Rood is a tall, taciturn man with a bulbous nose and acetylene torch scars on his left forearm that he earned when he worked as a welder. "Holdja for now," he tells Dad as he puts away his tools. "Storm coming. I'll finish later."

The rain from Hurricane Connie begins that mid-August afternoon and lasts several days and nights, though considerably short of forty. When the sun comes out, I look at the scratch I made on the car, then at the damage I caused to the garage. Then I spot Ripley's *Believe It Or Not*, still in the back seat. I take it out and bring it into the sun porch to read about floods, tornadoes, hurricanes, and other disasters whose devastation I find hard to believe.

Tom and Gerald are playing in the front yard when a box truck— the kind we called "half-trailer trucks"—stops in front of our house, its radiator steaming. The driver approaches my brothers and says something, and I put the book down and walk outside.

"...if I could get some water for my radiator," the man is saying.

"Yeah, OK," Tom volunteers, his speech greatly improved after months of speech therapy. "You got GMC, huh? That's a 1954 model, I know. What kind of engine you got?"

The man tells him, and they talk about engines and drive shafts and stuff for a few minutes, while Gerald, just turned five, seems to be taking it in. I uncoil the hose and turn on the spigot. No water comes out, and then I remember to turn the nozzle. When I do, it sprays Tom and Gerald and the driver, and I point it the other way. "Sorry," I mumble.

The man fills up his radiator, and I coil the hose back up against the south side of the house. The man fishes in his pocket and gives me two quarters. "Share that with your brothers," he says, climbing into the cab.

I put the money on top of Ripley, until I can figure out how to divide fifty cents by three. I never see the money again. I never see Ripley again. It is August 17, 1955, and the rain is starting again. Hurricane Diane is coming.

19

Tom is shaking me awake. "Jack, get up, there's a flood outside!" *He's up to his dumb little-brother tricks*, I think, *like the time he put Bayer Aspirin in the bottle of smoke-making pills that go in the smokestack of my Lionel locomotive*. But this time, he's not even funny. It's three in the morning or whatever. Does he think I'm going to jump out of bed, look out the window, smack my palm against my forehead and say, "Great joke, Tom! Hahaha! Let's wake Ann up and fool her too!"?

No, I'm going to go to the window, look out and see grass in the moonlight and cars going by on Route 44, and … OK, so there's no moon, and it's too dark and rainy to see the lawn, and it's too early for traffic, but … OK, so it sounds like there's a lot of water rushing by somewhere, but it's raining pretty hard and it's probably splashing in the puddles, but …

Holy cow. The house is in a river!

Apparently I'm the last one up. There is a dim, flickering glow from the stair landing, coming from the kitchen below, and some murmured gasps from Peggy downstairs.

"There's water down there," I tell Tom, looking back out the window.

"Well, that's what I told you!" he says. "Mr. Rood just came and woke us up."

"Where's everybody?"

"Downstairs."

The glow is from a candle Dad has placed on the kitchen table. Peggy is seated next to Dad, then Ann and Gerald in two other chairs around the table, as if they are waiting for Mom to serve pancakes with either syrup or butter but not both. The sound of rushing water is louder, but the black-and-white linoleum kitchen floor is still dry.

"Here he is," Tom announces as I make my entrance.

"Well, good morning, Jack," Dad says with a smile. "Welcome to the flood!"

"Where's Mom?" I say absently.

"Working," Peggy says. Her eyes are wild with a look I can't fathom.

"Don't you remember?" Dad says. "She's working at the convalescent home in Simsbury. Now listen, everyone. Russell Rood was just here. He said the water was up to his knees in our driveway. He barged into my room and told me to get all you kids up and out of the house. The water is rising fast."

"Well, how high can it get?" I ask.

"No one knows. But we—I have to make a decision, and—Jack, where are you going? Get away from the cellar door!"

But I've already opened it, wondering if there is any water in the cellar. Maybe there would be a foot or two on the basement floor, I am thinking.

What I see is not immediately comprehensible in the flickering candlelight. I see nothing but gray. Then I realize I am seeing a floor of gray water, almost perfectly level with the threshold. There isn't just a foot or two of water in the cellar. The cellar is one hundred percent submerged. My bicycle, the pump, Mom's washing machine, Mom's Mason jars of tomatoes, the Radio Flyer wagon—everything in the cellar is under eight feet of dirty, gray water.

"Dad, the cellar … the cellar is …."

"Close the door, Jack."

But it is too late. As though opening the door were like taking my finger out of a dike, water begins seeping over the threshold and through cracks in the linoleum, wetting our bare feet. In less than a minute a half-inch of water covers the floor. I close the door quickly, bracing for a now-you've-done-it reprimand that never comes.

"Upstairs!" Dad orders. "Go up now, and I'll be right up."

The five kids huddle on the dark upstairs landing and listen to Dad splashing around the downstairs rooms. He makes three or four trips up and down, bringing lamps and chairs and small end tables. Finally, he raids the refrigerator and bread drawer, bringing up a bottle of milk from Burdick's Dairy; a loaf of white bread that Ernie the Viking Bakery driver just delivered yesterday; a butter knife; and a jar of Hellmann's mayonnaise.

"It's knee-deep in the kitchen now," he says, barely ten minutes after I first let the water up from the cellar. "I don't think it will get much higher, but at least we'll have milk and sandwiches if we need breakfast later."

Four hours later—after we huddled in the boys' room and said the rosary, after the propane tanks were ripped by the current from the side of our house with a dreadful hissing noise, after the mayonnaise sandwiches were gone and we were still hungry and thirsty—four hours later, the water is still rising, the rain is still pelting down. I am looking out the south window, watching water gurgling up from the cellar window near the coiled hose and spigot. A horrible thought occurs to me.

"Dad?"

Dad is taking a break from piling furniture on top of beds and now sits on Tom's bed, staring out the window at the vast expanse of water covering the strawberry fields and surging around the now-completed skeleton house. "What is it, Jack?"

"The other day a truck driver stopped and Tom and Gerald and me gave him water for his radiator. I think I turned the hose off, but I'm not really sure."

"Oh, well, I wouldn't worry about that too much now."

"Well, OK. But I just wondered ... I mean ... do you think that could have caused the flood?"

Some children might have been hurt by the sound of Dad's laughter, but to me it is welcome. Dad hasn't laughed all morning, and now he can barely stop.

"Jack," Dad says wiping his eye under his glasses, "you didn't cause the flood, and you didn't let water up from the cellar."

"Oh. I thought I did something wrong."

"Well, you did. You said 'Tom and Gerald and me.' It's 'Tom and Gerald and I.'"

Now there is a screeching sound from the east side of the house. Peggy shouts, "The garage is going!" Everyone crowds around one of two windows, one in Peggy's room and one in Ann's, to watch the garage pull loose from the sun porch and tangle itself in utility wires. From Ann's room, Tom and I see the line go taut and the utility pole snap in two like a matchstick. The line gives off a bright blue spark as it hits the water.

"Did you see that?" I say.

Tom can only nod, still staring out the window.

Peggy and I sit on the top landing and watch the water climb the stairs. "I guess the train won't come today," I say.

Peggy stares at the rising water.

"And Old Man Mikoley, the guy who walks the tracks and picks up coal. He won't walk today, I bet."

Peggy keeps staring. Then she turns her head away from me.

"What's the matter?"

She stands up. "Do you think …?"

"What?"

"Nothing. I hope … I hope Mom …."

A crunching sound interrupts her. The north side of the house now has become darker than usual. Peggy runs to investigate.

"Minnie and George's house is right here! Right against our house!" she announces.

The white clapboards of Houghs' house are slowly bobbing up and down three feet from one of the master bedroom's windows. Out the other window we see the Houghs' upstairs window, perfectly aligned with ours. All appears dark and lifeless inside.

Dad climbs into the attic to check for weak spots in the roof, in case he needs to chop a hole and bring us even higher above the flood. He is cursing himself for not getting us out of the house while the water was still low. Weeks later, he will tell himself that he probably couldn't have done it. He would have had to carry two kids at a time across the road and into the woods, go back for two more, then go back for the last one. What if he didn't have time for the last one? "Which one would I have left behind?" he will ask.

Tom hears the tapping first. He looks out Dad's bedroom window and sees George Hough, huddled beside Minnie, holding a candle and tapping on their window. "Daddy!" Tom calls. "It's Minnie and George!"

Dad scurries back down the green, steel ladder—the one that used to belong to the swing set where Peggy broke her arm and I got stung by wasps—and carries it to his bedroom. He slides the window open. George slides his open. Rain slants in and soaks our floorboards. The flood roars like a waterfall. It is still rising, now almost to second floor level.

"George, hold on, we'll try this," he says, laying the ladder from our windowsill to theirs. The first and fifth rungs are missing, but the ladder is sturdy.

"John, lookit this!" George says. "The houses are right together, we can peek right into your house, you know?"

"Hehehe!" Minnie says.

"Come on over!" Dad says.

George's face falls. Minnie stops her nervous laughter and clears her throat.

"Well?" Dad says.

George whispers something to Minnie, and she shakes her head.

"John, we better not, you know?" George says. "We can't swim. And Minnie's afraid, you know? She might not fit, being heavy. I think we'll be all right here, you know?"

From the bowels of their floating home, stressed timbers let out a mournful groan.

"George, your house could float away at any minute. It's rocking now. Ours is still on the foundation."

George lowers his eyes. "We'll stay," he says.

Dad doesn't say a word. He pulls the ladder back inside. He climbs back to the attic, muttering under his breath, and I hear "...least of my Goddamn worries..." and "...my own skin, my kids, my house...." He is slamming things around in the attic.

Seven-year-old Ann is the one who stays by the window, talking almost nonstop to Minnie and George, getting them to change their minds. She runs into the hallway and shouts up to the attic, "Dad! They want to come now!"

Again, Dad scurries back down, lays the ladder between the windowsills. George wobbles across on hands and knees, as I steady the ladder from one side, Dad from the other. The rungs are hard against George's knees and shins, and he says, "Ouch! Ouch! Ouch!" the entire three-foot journey.

Safe inside our house, George coaxes Minnie across the chasm, as water ten feet deep laps at her knees. She is less complaining of the trip than George was, but clearly more frightened, giggling nervously and trembling. Two feet above her, the eaves of both houses form a canopy against the rain, but inches below her the opaque gray flood makes gurgling snatches at her knees. Both Dad and George reach out the window to steady her and reassure her. When she's halfway over, they pull her in and she rolls most unladylike into our house. She clings briefly to George and squeezes her eyes shut, lets out a long, ragged sigh.

Suddenly, George is back on the ladder! "I have to get some things," he says.

"George, what the hell are you doing?" Dad shouts—the only time he completely loses his patience this day. George has disappeared back into the darkness of his house, as Minnie screams for him to come back. He finally reappears with case after case of Winston cigarettes, dozens of cartons, which he slides across. Finally, he crawls over again, just as the water is seeping through the floorboards of our second floor.

"Into the attic!" Dad orders us kids. Minnie—after relieving herself in the empty Burdick Dairy milk bottle—follows us up. George says he is claustrophobic, so he and Dad stay below, sloshing around on the second floor. They are the only witnesses to the spectacle of Houghs' house rolling around the front of ours, scraping against the maple tree, and splitting in half. The top half smashes into Bertha Atkins's tarpaper house. The bottom half, we learn later, disintegrates against the Schlossers' barn.

They have come over just in time. No one could have survived the wreck of the Hough house.

A motorboat sputters down Route 44. Mr. Krom from Pine Meadow is trying to rescue people. He shouts to Dad that he'll be right back. He doesn't return. We learn later that his boat capsizes as he is rescuing a man from a roof. They swim to safety.

Planes and helicopters circle and hover. Dad and George wave handkerchiefs out the window. "Why don't they land?" George asks stupidly.

"On what airport?" Dad says.

I have to pee. Dad lets me down from the attic, and I stand on a hamper below the scuttle door. I start to pee into the flooded landing, when I hear shattering glass and see water coursing through a broken window on the north side, where the Houghs' house used to be. It is the only time I am fearful, and I am no longer able to add my own water to the millions of gallons below me. I stand dumbly watching as Dad wades to the window on the south side and smashes it, letting the current flow through the house. I peer around the corner and see beds floating in the boys' room.

The rain slows; the water crests, goes down a few inches, then climbs back up again, like a wild day on Wall Street. Finally it sluices down the stairwell as though a plug has been pulled. In five minutes, it drops a foot. We learn later that a logjam at the Satan's Kingdom Bridge, where Johnny Ryan lives, finally gave way, allowing water to cascade through the narrow gorge.

Now we are down from the attic, and there is an inch of mud on the upstairs floor. A helicopter is blowing the willow branches around above us. The walloping sound is deafening. Dad climbs out the window he smashed and onto the sun porch roof, where he sits and signals to the helicopter. Five fingers with one hand, two with the other, then he jerks a thumb toward the window. Seven people inside, he is trying to say. I see the helicopter pilot, wearing a red baseball cap, shaking his head and flying off. The willow trees would have made a rescue impossible, especially a rescue of eight people.

Minutes later, Peggy and I wander into our parents' bedroom. Dad is taking pictures off the wall. George is gazing out the window he and Minnie have crawled through, a blank expression on his face. He seems to be looking directly at the spot where his house once stood. Peggy and I look at each other, both no doubt thinking the same thought: *What goes through a man's mind after he has lost everything?*

George turns to Dad and says casually, "Well, it ain't rainin', John, but there's still a hell of a lot of water."

Peggy's eyes widen. *Is that it?* we both think. *Is that all he can say?*

By midafternoon, the water is nearly gone. The mud gets thicker with each step we take downstairs. A neighbor, a Mr. Goodman, has shown up, offering to help. Dad asks him to take us kids to the convent about two miles away. As I trudge out of the house, I want to stop and survey the horrible sight, but Dad makes us all step lively. What I do see, in the five seconds it takes me to walk through the kitchen and out the sun porch, is this: mud two feet thick on the floor, the electric clock on the wall stopped at three-twenty-five, and the entire east wall of the sun porch gone, where it was attached to the garage. The garage that Mr. Rood had just repaired. The garage that held the hayloft filled with the Edison phonograph, John McCormack records, and barn swallow nests. In the yard are puddles and deep holes. The road is torn up. Dad delivers us to Mr. Goodman and says, "Go with Mr. Goodman. He's a good man."

"Aren't you coming?" Peggy wants to know.

"I'll be along. I'll see if I can stay with Father Byrne at the rectory next door to the convent. Now go." Then one final attempt at humor: "But remember: look both ways before crossing the street."

Later, Dad will tell us of his friend Mr. Miller's visit a few minutes after we left. Mr. Miller was from Pine Meadow, a half mile north. Whenever they got together, they offered each other a beer. Dad thought this should be no exception. He opened the Frigidaire and water poured out of it. Then he reached for a bottle of Miller High Life and pulled the bottle opener from its nail on the wall, where it had been submerged in filthy water for seven hours, and opened a Miller for Mr. Miller.

"Cheers, Bill," he said. "So, how was *your* day?"

20

The sun is finally breaking through. Steam is rising from puddles. The Flood of '55 is evaporating.

We follow Mr. Goodman up the logging road where Mr. Bills used to drive tractors and trucks to maintain his spring. We veer off the path and trudge barefoot through muddy, hilly terrain overgrown with prickly vegetation. Mr. Goodman carries Gerald most of the way. We reach the high clearing overlooking Shepard's Field, a pasture that is still flooded. Route 44 curves around the far edge of the field. Two or three cars and a couple of town trucks are stopped along the road, but we see no people near them.

"Let's get to the railroad tracks," Mr. Goodman says. We skirt the edge of the wooded area on the west edge of Shepard's Field and reach the track bed just beyond where it crosses Route 44 and hugs the base of Jones's Mountain in Pine Meadow. "Watch out for broken glass," Mr. Goodman says. "Keep your feet on the ties."

Peggy begins the chant, "Keep your feet on the ties, keep your feet on the ties," planting her left foot on the word *feet* and her right foot on the word *ties*.

A few steps north of the Millers' house, a gully has undermined the tracks, which are sagging over a deep ravine. Mr. Goodman helps us down and around the ravine and back onto the tracks on the other side.

"I'm hungry," Ann says.

"Be quiet," Peggy says. "All you do is complain."

"I'm hungry," Ann says again.

"And in the attic, all you could say was, 'I'm itchy.' Over and over again. 'I'm itchy, I'm itchy, I'm itchy.' *Everybody* was itchy. It was from the insulation."

"I'm still itchy. And hungry," Ann says. "I'm itchy, I'm hungry, I'm thirsty, I'm tired."

"All right, kids, don't fight, we're almost there," Mr. Goodman says.

We reach the black steel trestle that spans the still turgid Farmington River. To the left, a spur continues along the base of Jones's Mountain, parallel to and overlooking Route 44. We take the spur. The stretch of highway below us, between the village center and the trestle, is called The Dugway, because long ago the road had been dug out of the base of the mountain for easier access to Pine Meadow. A concrete dike about twenty-five feet high was built to separate river from road. Today, the dike still stands, but the river has met the road anyway and gave new meaning to The Dugway: the roadbed has been torn into great slabs of crazily angled concrete, as if a giant steel fist has dug into it.

Tom bends down and picks up a round can of Copenhagen snuff from the track bed. "What's this?" he asks.

"Put it down," Mr. Goodman says. "That looks like Mr. Mikoley's. He must have come through here a day or so ago and lost it. Leave it there. He'll no doubt be back and he'll find it."

In the center of town, Mr. Goodman leads us off the tracks and onto Town Hill Road, to our left. We pass Shea's Funeral Home, which will be busy in the next few days, and curl around the Immaculate Conception Cemetery, which will have some new tenants soon. We trudge wearily up the hill and past Saint Mary's School, where all of us but Gerald are now enrolled. Saint Joseph's Convent, which houses the nuns who teach us, is next door. "Wait here," Mr. Goodman says.

We stand by a fire hydrant at the end of the walkway that leads to the convent. Mr. Goodman climbs the steps and knocks at the wide, white front door.

I am trying now to see ourselves as Sister Saint George must have seen us when she answered the door. She would have listened to Mr. Goodman's apologetic greeting and then followed the sweep of his hand that indicated five children standing twenty yards away. After a gasp, punctuated by a hand that flew involuntarily to her mouth, the black-habited housekeeper nun would have recognized the Sheedy children. And although she must certainly have been aware of the flood that had just ravaged the town in the valley below her, she must have wondered why the normally well-dressed Sheedy children now appeared before her barefoot, in pajamas, dirty, tired, and hungry at four o'clock in the afternoon of an August day.

"They're homeless," Mr. Goodman says. "Their home was destroyed."

"Lord help them. Bring them in," Sister Saint George says. But as we approach the steps, she says, "Wait!" She turns and calls into the convent, "Mother Remigius! Can you come here, please?"

A short, stocky nun appears. She is the Mother Superior, Sister Mary Remigius. She surveys us with a quick, sharp eye. "Well, bring them in, Sister," she commands, her eyes still boring into us.

Instinctively, we wipe our feet, but the chain-and-rubber mat scratches our soles. "Quickly!" Mother Remigius says, as if we are responding late to the bell that calls us in from recess. "Where are your clothes?" she demands as we huddle in the foyer.

After an awkward silence, Mr. Goodman says, "Mr. Sheedy will bring them. The children had to leave the house immediately because it is unsafe."

"Was the house washed away?" Sister Saint George asks.

"No, it is still standing. But the flood severely damaged it."

"Water in the basement?" Mother Remigius says.

"Yes, ma'am. Sister, I mean. But also in the main living areas."

"Good Lord," Sister Saint George says. "Some damage, perhaps, to the carpets and downstairs furniture?"

"Yes, Sister. Actually, Sister, the water completely destroyed everything in the basement and downstairs areas and much of the upstairs bedroom areas."

"Excuse me, did you say upstairs? How can that be?" Sister Saint George says.

"Sister, Mr. Sheedy told me the water reached higher than two feet on the second floor. The children were forced into the attic. The Houghs' house left its foundation and crashed into the Sheedys' house, and Mr. Sheedy rescued the Houghs. I am very sorry to have to come to you, but these children have no place to sleep tonight. Mr. Sheedy wonders if you can find temporary shelter for them here."

Mother Remigius's eyes have never left us. I am beginning to feel the way I feel when walking through DeLott's Department Store downtown, with old Mr. DeLott following me through the aisles, drumming his fingers on the shelves to let me know he is watching me. But now, as I look back up at her, I see Mother Remigius is biting her bottom lip and her eyes are shiny. She turns quickly away and whispers commands to Sister Saint George.

Soon, the entire population of nuns surrounds us, a half dozen of them, Gothic arches in black and white. They are asking us questions about the flood. Where is our father? Where is our mother? Do we have any clothing? Have we eaten anything? What kind of damage has the flood caused?

We do our best to answer the questions, but we are tired and in a kind of shock. We never notice when Mr. Goodman takes his leave. I don't even recall when Dad arrives with a cardboard carton of rumpled clothes he salvaged from an overturned and soggy chest of drawers. But I do recall the meal of grilled cheese sandwiches and hot tomato soup Sister Saint George served us. (It was Friday. No meat.) And, to my lasting chagrin, I recall the hot bath that Mother Remigius chose to administer to me in person. I am nine years and six months old today, and capable of bathing myself, but Mother Remigius insists on washing me. I have just survived a devastating flood, and now she is afraid to leave me alone in a wash tub filled with hot water. "I can do it myself!" I say.

"I don't mind," she says. She is smiling. Her voice is calm.

For the next three years, while Mother Remigius presides over my fourth-, fifth-, and sixth-grade classes, I am embarrassed to recall that she has seen me naked. Only decades later do I grant her the understanding that she was acting out a larger role than simply scrubbing my skinny body with a sudsy wash cloth. She has seen me hungry, thirsty, cast out from my home. She has fed me, given me drink, given me shelter. Now she is preparing to clothe me.

"For I was hungry and you gave me to eat; I was thirsty and you gave me to drink; I was a stranger and you took me in," Mother Remigius no doubt was reciting to herself, from Matthew 25; "naked and you covered me."

21

We sleep on the floor in two downstairs front rooms of the convent. In the dark, there is the sound of ticking clocks and the murmur of nuns praying upstairs in the chapel. I wander the halls in the night looking for a bathroom and almost stumble into the room of a sleeping nun.

Life at the convent is unremarkable. The nuns try to find entertainment for us and introduce us to Chinese checkers. Is this a glimpse into convent life? Do nuns play Chinese checkers when all their prayers and chores are done?

Meals are simple, forgettable. Toast, cereal and juice for breakfast. Sandwiches and soup for lunch. I have no memory of Saturday night's supper.

The highlight of Saturday—the only part I vividly recall—is queueing up with Dad for our typhoid shots at the town hall. The lines meander from the Finast grocery store on Bridge Street (now missing its bridge), past the hotel entrance, past the Kandy Kitchen on Main Street, and into the old town hall, where Dr. Markwald is busily sticking everyone with needles in the arm.

"Doctor, I'm glad you're safe," Dad says.

"My house is ruined," Dr. Markwald says.

"I'm sorry."

"But we're safe. Left or right?"

"What?"

"Roll up one sleeve or another, I don't have all day."

Dad takes his medicine and hangs around while we get our shots. "When will the water be safe to drink?" Dad asks.

"Peggy, left or right?" Dr. Markwald says.

"Right," Peggy says.

"Maybe it's already safe."

"What do you mean?" Dad asks.

"You!" Dr. Markwald says, peering down at me. "You didn't kick that bucket yet? Left or right?"

"Right," I say, because that's what Peggy chose.

"Do you have a cat?" the doctor asks Dad.

"Yes, if she hasn't run away."

"Ann, left or right?"

"Left," Ann says.

"When power comes back on, draw some water for the cat," Dr. Markwald says.

"Ouch!" Ann says. "That hurt!"

"That's not my fault, you said left. Tom, left or right?"

"Right," says Tom, who is no fool.

"Then give some water from your well to the cat," Dr. Markwald says. "Gerald, left or right?"

"Um, I don't know."

"Roll up your right sleeve. John, I don't have time to test everybody's wells. If your cat dies, don't drink the water. Mrs. Langevin, left or right?"

Except for this excursion for the typhoid shot, we are not allowed to wander far afield. The shoes we kicked off two long nights ago, before the flood, are still under our beds—waterlogged and ruined.

"Are you ready for Mass?" Mother Remigius asks us on Sunday morning.

"We have no shoes," Peggy says.

"Jesus will not mind that. And your father is waiting outside for you."

Dad is dressed in baggy gray trousers, the kind he liked to wear when working in the yard—the yard that is now littered with fallen willow trees, splintered lumber from the garage, and the Houghs' commode. He is wearing shoes, but they are muddy.

"Did you sleep OK?" he asks Peggy.

"No. I keep hearing the flood in my head. Rushing water, all night long. And then Mom's voice, crying."

"Where's the car?" Gerald asks.

"Our Chrysler is ruined," Dad says.

"But Mom has the Chevy, right?" Tom asks.

Dad takes a breath and lets it out in a whimper. "Yes," he finally says.

We walk down the hill again, past the schoolhouse, the cemetery, the funeral home.

"I should have gone to confession last night," Dad says. "But I didn't."

"Why?" Peggy says.

"Why didn't I?"

"No, why should you have gone?"

"Oh, a lot of reasons. And I have no excuse. My confessor sleeps in the room next to mine."

"But why?" Peggy insists.

"Well, for one thing, I ate meat on Friday."

We are silent. Today is Sunday, August 21. Friday was August 19, the day of the flood. The day we had mayonnaise sandwiches.

"We didn't eat meat that day," I say. "We didn't eat much of anything."

"No, you didn't, I'm sure. But I did."

"It's a sin to eat meat on Fridays, right Dad?" Ann says.

"There was one piece of salami in the refrigerator Friday morning, before I brought the bread and mayonnaise upstairs. I ate it. I didn't even think about it being Friday. It was there, and I ate it. And I brought you mayonnaise sandwiches."

"But that's a sin, isn't it?" Ann asks.

Dad just keeps walking, looking down at his shoes.

The Immaculate Conception Church is overflowing with people at the eight o'clock Mass, but Dad leads us up the center aisle to our usual pew near the front. The carpeting is soft and a little prickly on our bare feet. All around us are men dressed in suits and ties, women in dresses and hats. There must be other flood victims who are dressed as shabbily as we are, but we don't notice them.

"This is a sad time for us all," Father Byrne says from the pulpit. "Our community may have lost eight souls, and many more are homeless. Some are missing." He glances at the six Sheedys, then looks quickly away. He says nothing about us, but everyone knows we are temporary wards of the parish, and that Mrs. Sheedy is missing.

"The Krohner family lost their newborn baby," Father Byrne says. "It was swept from Mrs. Krohner's arms when their house was floating away in Satan's Kingdom."

My eyes widen. Just this summer we went to a clambake at the Krohners'. Their biggest tragedy up to now was when Mrs. Krohner lost her wedding ring in the swimming pool at that clambake, and they had to drain the pool to find it. She found her baby the same way, but there was no rejoicing. The flood drained away and there was the baby—lifeless and snagged on barbed wire five miles downstream.

"Their neighbors, the Bouchards, lost four family members," Father Byrne continues. "The mother and both daughters are lost. And a cousin."

Peggy and I look at each other. "Carol and Linda!" Peggy whispers. "From our Red Cross swimming class!"

Mrs. Bouchard wanted her daughters to learn to swim because she never did.

Father Byrne tells us about two town workers who died when their truck slid into the river. "And Michael Mikoley, the man we all have seen walking along the railroad tracks, is still missing," he says.

I look at Tom. Old Man Mikoley will never come back for his can of Copenhagen. His body is found days later, three hundred yards behind our house.

We don't go to Communion. We don't want people to see the soles of our feet. Dad understands, and he doesn't go either.

As we file out the center aisle, Mr. Roberge takes Dad aside. "John, your children have no shoes."

"I know that, Joe."

"But I have a shoe store."

"Yes, Joe, and as soon as I get back on—"

"John, listen to me. Right now, just follow me to the shoe store. I will give them and you each a pair of shoes." He glances at our feet. "And socks, too."

The fittings for all six of us take only twenty minutes. Dad offers some crumpled bills to Mr. Roberge, who declines them. We feel taller, prouder, as we click our way out the door. On the sidewalk, other townspeople are lined up, some in muddy shoes, some in socks, some barefoot. Mr. Roberge has free shoes for all of them.

The next day, Monday, Dad collects us again from the convent and leads us down the hill to DeLott's Department Store. He tells Mr. DeLott to put aside a push broom and a few other items so he can clear the mud out of our house. Then we follow Dad back up Route 44, past the Immaculate Conception Church on Central Avenue, past Shea's Funeral Home on Town Hill Road, past a 1951 Chevy that has slowed to a stop at a bend in the road just below the convent. The woman driving it is wearing a nurse's cap. She sees us and rolls down the window. "John! Oh, thank God!" she calls.

Dad stops and stares. Mom opens the car door and stands next to it. We stand and watch our parents embrace in the morning sun.

22

Peggy and I are playing treasure hunt in the spring of 1956 when the Baxters begin moving into the house that Mr. Bills built. "10 paces south from willow tree nearest road. Dig," the piece of paper says in Peggy's neat cursive. As I begin pacing, the Daly Moving & Storage van drives past and slows down, then turns into the driveway next door.

"Pay attention," Peggy says. "You're taking too big steps. You're supposed to pace."

"There's a moving van," I say. "And anyway, what's a pace? Isn't it like a giant step?"

"No, it's just a normal step. Is Bertha moving?"

We halt the game and gaze across the strawberry field. There is a picture of a blue globe on the side of the van, with longitude and latitude lines and the slogan, "The world moves daily ... Daly moves the world." Two muscular, potbellied men in blue uniforms begin carrying end tables and easy chairs.

"It's not Bertha," I say. "Someone's moving into the new house."

I resume pacing, even though I lost count. I know where to dig. Right in the middle of the driveway, where the dirt is a different color. Three inches down is a Kellogg's Corn Flakes box top, the kind you need two of, plus twenty-five cents in coin, to send away for a model of an orange

North American Van Lines truck. On the back of the box top Peggy has written, "22 paces east. Turn left. 13 paces north. Dig."

Twenty minutes and seventeen clues later, I am back at the willow tree. I dig. "Look up," the clue inside the Hellmann's mayonnaise jar says. In the crotch of the tree is a Maxwell House coffee can. I shinny up the tree, and the can rattles all the way down. A cloth covers the opening, held in place by a rubber band. "Open it," Peggy says.

Inside is an onyx-beaded rosary with a heavy, sterling silver crucifix. "Wow!" I say. "Where did you get this?"

"Do you like it?"

"Well, yeah. But—well, thanks."

"It's OK. It's Mom's, so don't lose it. You can use it for my treasure when you make clues for me tomorrow."

"Oh. Well, yeah, sure."

"You thought I was giving it to you? It's just a game," she says, and I wonder why she is suddenly impatient with me. Is it because we are in that forty-eight-day window when we are both ten years old? Or is something else going on?

Peggy and I still play together, but I no longer can quite tune into her thoughts. Since that Monday after the flood, when we were reunited with Mom, Peggy is either cheerful and outgoing, or sullen and withdrawn. She cries quietly in her room. Once I overhear her on the phone with a girlfriend, saying, "When Dad and Mom were hugging that day, I ran over to them and tried to push Dad away, shouting, 'Mom! Mom!' and I hugged her around the waist. I must have been crying. I heard her telling Dad that Civil Defense told her there was still one bridge over Nepaug Reservoir she could use to get to New Hartford. But I thought my mother had died, I really did!"

Now we look across the strawberry field at the potbellied men wiping their faces with identical blue kerchiefs. I imagine the kerchiefs are embroidered with darker blue globes of the world. Almost in unison they hitch up their pants and scratch their crotches, then climb back into the cab of the van, one on either side.

The Baxters arrive the next morning: a slim, Ozzie-and-Harriett couple in their late thirties with a boy named Bruce and his younger brother Greg. Mom invites them over for coffee.

"I thought I saw you Sunday after Mass at the Marble Pharmacy," Mom says. "What did you think of Father Byrne's sermon about not judging others?"

"Oh, we're not Catholics," Mrs. Baxter says. "We attend services at the North Congregational Church right near yours. Services let out at about the same time, it seems."

"Oh, I see," Mom says. "Well, of course that's fine. As Father Byrne said, we should not judge others, right? Mr. Baxter, what do you do?"

"Hmm? Oh, I call myself a mariners' specialist," he says with a grin. "Do you know what that is?"

"Well, not exactly. A cook in the Navy?" Mom says.

"Nope. You would have judged me wrong. I sell boats and outboard motors. Johnson and Evinrude mostly. Baxter's Boats and Marine. The sign will go up in a day or so. I'll have my showroom downstairs from Mrs. Atkins's apartment."

"In Mr. Bills's old workshop?" I say.

"That's what I understand," he says.

"Dad, I can show Jack where your boats will be," says Bruce. He is about a year younger than I am, but, like most of my peers, two inches taller. Unlike my peers, he is skinny, like me.

"That would be nice," Mr. Baxter says. "If it's all right with Mrs. Sheedy, of course."

"Of course," Mom says.

"But Greg stays here, right?" Bruce says. "He's not supposed to run around a lot anyway."

Mrs. Baxter looks at Mom. "Greg has a heart murmur," she says. Then, with a too-bright smile, she adds, "But he's just fine, aren't you Greg? You can stay here while your brother shows the place to Jack, all right, Greg?"

Seven-year-old Greg, who was coloring at the kitchen table, wriggles off his chair and runs to his mother. "Wanna go outside," he says.

"Later," his mother says. "Don't excite yourself, now."

Bruce and I run across the strawberry patch, where there are still rotting planks from the Houghs' splintered house. We walk into the old workshop, past the iron vat where Mr. Bills used to dunk Peggy and me in the icy spring water. The vat is empty and rusting, the once-constant flow of spring water halted after last summer's flood washed away portions of Mr. Bills's aqueduct. The eastern area of the workshop, which once was a garage for Mr. Bills's tractor, is empty now, the concrete floor swept clean, the workbenches and toolboxes gone.

"It's all changed," I say.

"You mean you've been here before?" Bruce says.

"I live next door," I remind him. "Peggy and I played here a lot with Mr. Bills."

"Oh. Anyway, Dad took a lot of stuff to the dump. It looked like it was all ruined by rain or something."

"The flood," I say.

"Oh, right. Anyway, everything smelled like a sewer."

He shows me where the boats will be, then takes me back outside to show me his yard. He doesn't know why there are cement slabs near the edge of the railroad tracks until I tell him that Mr. Bills had a barn and chicken coops there, but the flood took them away. I know more about his yard than he does.

"Dad's going to put a swing set here," Bruce says, pointing to the spot where Russell and Jessie Rood's trailer stood before the flood carried it away like an empty soup can. "But Greg can't swing on it."

"Why not?"

"Greg's sick. Don't tell him, but he's gonna die."

"Really? When?"

"Some day. Pretty soon. Mom says his heart mumbles or something."

We both find this fascinating: a real live person that we both know is going to die "pretty soon." We sit, hidden in tall grass, and he tells me about trips to hospitals, doctors, drug stores. He describes amber bottles of medicine, pamphlets with pink-and-black drawings of a heart, pronouncements by doctors that he "should not exert himself." Little Greg Baxter is going to die. And he doesn't even know it.

23

A year after the flood, we visit Aunt Jane again in upstate New York. This time, she notices that my eyes are almost as blue as Gerald's and asks Mom if I can stay on the farm for a couple weeks after the rest of the family leaves.

I crouch between rows of pole beans beside Aunt Jane, who keeps smiling at me. I am helping her cultivate, tossing the weeds into a paper grocery bag.

"Your Mom tells me her kitchen is almost completely renovated," she says.

"Yeah, it was in the home show and everything." I tell her about how Dad got a small business loan, secured by the hearing aid business, and how some of that money helped with the kitchen. "We got a refrigerator and some furniture from the Red Cross," I say. "And a little money from friends and relatives. The house was a real mess after the flood."

"You missed some lambs-quarters," she says, pointing to a leafy weed.

"Oh, right. Mom saves these."

"She doesn't weed them out?"

"Well yeah, but she lets them grow a little first, so she can boil them. They taste like spinach."

"That's your Mom, all right. She's a McElhone."

I'm not sure what being a McElhone really means, except that it used to be Mom's and Aunt Jane's last name.

"How did you like living with your Doyle cousins in Simsbury?" she asks.

"OK. Better than the convent. And they bought us some clothes. But after a couple weeks, it was good to go home, even if it was still smelly and dirty."

"I can't even imagine how it must have been."

"You didn't get a flood here, right Aunt Jane? You're way up, and way away from cities too. How come you moved here?"

Instead of answering, she hands me the paper bag. "Time to empty this in the composting pile. Want to do the honors?"

I carry the half-full bag to the fenced-off compost heap at the edge of the cow pasture.

"It must have been dreadful for your parents," she says when I return.

"Well yeah, for all of us."

"But they're your parents. They're the ones who want to keep you safe. To care for you. Nothing's worse in the world than to lose a child."

"They didn't, though."

"Well, still. Hey, why are you pulling that up?"

"It's a weed."

"It's lambs-quarters. From now on, just for you, it's a vegetable."

That night, Aunt Jane organizes a family card game of Michigan Rummy. She divvies pennies up among all the kids, including me, and we try to play the money cards that have piles of coins on them. We get to keep all our winnings, too.

"Two of clubs," Ben says, laying it down.

"Three and four," Jim Junior says.

"Five," I say.

"Six, seven, eight, nine," Aunt Jane says.

Silence. No one has the ten of clubs.

"OK," Aunt Jane says. "I go again. Eight of hearts. That's my lowest."

"Nine and ten," Barbara says.

"Jack and queen," says Nancy.

"King and ace!" I say, scraping about eight pennies off the ace of hearts. "Oh, and I'm out, so I get the kitty, too!"

"Great job, Jack," Aunt Jane says. "You're as good a card player as any of the Eight Snuffs."

"It's just a game of luck," I say. "Anyway, why do you call your kids Eight Snuffs? They don't do snuff, do they?"

"No, no. After I had the last one, I told your Uncle Jim, 'Eight is enough.'"

"Yeah," Ben says. "And Barbara was only six and thought it sounded like 'Eight Snuff.'"

"It's enough, and it's not enough," Aunt Jane says. Then she quietly deals another hand.

During the day, I help Ben with the chores—milking the cows, gathering eggs, feeding the livestock—but afterwards, I get to do what I want. Ben has friends he hangs out with, and so I'm left by myself a lot. On this hot August day, I sit by the fire pond and pick up a white kitten, one of dozens of cats that hang around the farm. The minute I pick her up, the heat bug starts up, and I look up in the trees, searching for it. As always, it's invisible. But my distraction is enough to allow the kitten to wriggle free.

"Come back, kitty!" I say. "Here, kitty!"

The kitten is slow, and I catch her in the tall grass pretty easily. She reminds me of Frosty, Peggy's white cat with black spots that we kept with us in the attic during the flood. "Little known fact," Dad said as he handed the cat up to us. "Cats can swim. They don't like to, and they wouldn't do well in this raging flood. But they can swim if they have to."

Cats can swim.

The heat bug is just winding down now, ending its minute-long buzz. I hold the kitten out over a shallow part of the pond and gently set her in.

She scrambles out in a panic, shaking her fur and stumbling blindly toward the house. I catch up with her and carry her back toward the pond. "You can do it," I say, rubbing the kitten's matted fur. I gently toss her out about five feet. She gyrates in the air, lands with a sploosh, and immediately paddles back to shore, straight toward me. I scoop her up. "Good kitty!" I say. "Good job! You can swim!"

I toss her out again, this time about ten feet, and again she heads straight back to me, keeping me in her sights all the way. I am her deliverer. She relies on me. She is enjoying her swimming lesson. She will never be afraid of the water again.

"Good kitty!" I say again, feeling her heart drumming in her little chest. "One more time. Here you go!"

The kitten sails out toward the center of the pond, silhouetted against the bright sky, as the heat bug starts up once again. The kitten lands with a loud splash, goes under for a half second, then comes up and thrashes around, looking for me. She paddles first one way, then the other way, then finally sees me and starts to paddle toward me. "Good kitty!" I say.

"Come on!" The heat bug drones on. The kitten's eyes are wide and staring straight at me. She starts to swim toward me, then stops suddenly, her body twitches once, and she starts to sink. "Kitty!" I shout. "Come on! Swim!"

But she is not swimming. She is floating face down, not moving a muscle. *Oh my God!* I think. *Oh my God!* I pull off my shoes, my shirt, my pants. Naked except for my underpants, I wade in—it's only up to my chest at its deepest—and scoop up the lifeless kitten and bring it to shore, just fifteen feet away. I lay her down in the grass and push on her sides, trying to force water out of her lungs, trying to perform some sort of artificial respiration. It doesn't work. The white kitten is a soaking rag, limp and dead. I killed her. I killed a kitten.

Tears come to my eyes as the heat bug finishes its racket. I pull my clothes on over my wet skin. I have to tell Aunt Jane.

I find her in a row of pole beans, under a giant, wide-brimmed white hat. "Hi there, Jack! Looking for more lambs-quarters?"

"Um, no. Um, Aunt Jane?"

She glances down at me. "What is it, Jack? Why are you soaking wet?"

"I—I didn't mean it. I didn't mean to. But one of your kittens? I thought she could learn to swim. So I—I put her in the pond, but she drowned. I didn't mean it. I'm sorry!"

"Oh." She turns back to picking her pole beans.

"Did you hear me?"

"Hm? Yes, I heard you. You didn't mean it, but you drowned the kitten. Don't worry about that."

"But it was—just a kitten. Just a little kitten!"

"Exactly. Just a kitten. Not a person, right? It's one less cat we'll have to do away with."

I was expecting one of two possible reactions. One, Aunt Jane will turn on me and yell, *How could you be so stupid?* Or, two, Aunt Jane will drop her bucket of beans and scoop me up in her arms and say, *Oh you poor thing, you must feel terrible!*

Either of the other two reactions would have helped me get over it. Instead, I dream of it every night for months. A white kitten, one who trusted me, starts to paddle toward me, then takes another look at her friend and savior, the boy who hurled it into the pond three times. *Why,* thinks the kitten, *should I try to swim? He will only throw me back.* And she puts her head into the water and inhales.

24

"Here's your first clue," I tell Bruce. I hand him a note card that says, "Go 8 paces from Sheedy mailbox toward Sheedy maple tree. Dig."

"Is this a game?" he asks.

"Treasure hunt," I say. "It's fun."

Bruce glances around, a bit bewildered. "Where's—?"

"Our mailbox. Right by the road," I say.

"No, I mean … where's the maple tree?"

I point to the only maple tree in sight, at the north edge of our property.

"Oh, OK, that's a maple?" He grins, looks embarrassed. "Hey, I know an Evinrude motor from a Johnson, but don't ask me about trees, OK?"

We laugh. "Hey Bruce, maybe I could tell an Evinrude from a Johnson if I read the name on the motor, you know?" And we laugh some more.

"OK, so eight paces. One. Two—"

"No, paces, not giant steps," I say. "Just, you know, walk."

"OK. This looks like it. Does your dad know you dug up his lawn?"

"No, and you're not going to tell, right? Anyway, I just lifted the whole, you know, grass and dirt and all with one shovelful and replaced it. You can't tell."

"Oh, like a golfer? Replacing the divots?" he says.

"What's that mean?" I say.

"When you swing too low and your club digs up the grass on the golf course, you know? You're supposed to replace the divot—the bunch of grass and dirt—so it looks nice again."

"OK, divots and outboard motors. But I still know more about trees!" We burst out laughing.

The note under the divot tells him to walk "24 paces toward the abandoned well" at the edge of what once was Houghs' property and dig in Mom's cucumber patch. The note there tells him to "walk 72 paces toward the gaping hole in the ground where Lyn Gas once stood." The final note says, "Look in your mailbox."

"My mailbox? I'm walking all around Puddletown just so I can look in my own mailbox?"

"So you're saying you're not having fun?" I tease.

"No, this is great," he says, starting toward his mailbox. "You coming?"

"Right behind you," I say, but something has caught my eye. From the living room window of our house, a curtain moves. I squint at it, but it is still.

I catch up to Bruce, who is running toward his mailbox. Inside is the business envelope I have stolen from Dad's stationery, with "Radioear of Hartford" printed on the return address corner.

"A letter from your dad?" he laughs.

"Not really. Open it."

He takes out a miraculous medal with a picture of Mary stepping on a snake. Around the picture are the words, "O Mary, conceived without sin, pray for us who have recourse to thee."

Bruce starts to laugh, then thinks better of it and tries to keep an expressionless face, just nodding, not knowing what to say. There is just an idea of a smile at the corners of his mouth.

"It's not much," I admit.

"No, it's ... thanks," he says. "You know, I'll keep it."

"I mean, I know you're Protestant," I say. "But I just thought. Well, I thought you'd want to know, for instance, that Catholics were here first, that's all. Protestant means people protested against the Catholics and started another religion."

"Really?"

"I gotta get home," I say. "But I could tell you more later. What do you think?"

"I think we're even now," he says, finally laughing. "You know Catholics and trees. I know divots and motors."

That afternoon Peggy and I watch Mickey Mouse Club. It's Wednesday, Anything Can Happen Day, which is really just a bunch of reruns from earlier shows. Peggy sits in the corner of the couch with her feet tucked under her, hugging a cushion, staring straight at Goofy, not even laughing when I laugh. When the show is over, she gets up without speaking.

At the supper table I tell everyone about the treasure hunt Bruce and I had, and Dad and Mom think it's great that I have a new friend. Peggy says nothing.

When I get into bed that night, I find a note on my pillow, written on Peggy's lavender stationery. "Walk 7 paces to window nearest porch," it says.

On the windowsill is another note: "Look in top dresser drawer."

In the dresser drawer is the final note: "This was OUR GAME!!!"

25

"This may take a while," Dad tells Peggy and me. "I'll drop you off at the skating rink."

It's a Saturday in September 1956, and Peggy and I are riding with Dad to Waterbury, where he has to fix a hearing aid at a customer's house. He double-parks in front of the huge brick building and leads us inside. The walls are dark wood, the noise is enormous, a never-ending rumbling of wheels.

"This should be enough. I'll be back in about two hours," Dad says. He waves a ten-dollar bill toward us. Peggy and I both reach for it. Dad finally gives it to Peggy. "Well, I guess you're both old enough to be responsible for the money, but Peggy is still older."

"Only until February nineteenth," I remind him with a smile. "Then we'll both be eleven."

"For not even seven weeks," Peggy says. She's smiling, but she's also insistent.

"My Irish twins," Dad says. "You're growing up too fast."

We watch the back of his fedora as he walks out. Peggy pays for the skate rental, laces up without a word to me and glides easily along the hardwood rink. She is a whole head taller than I am, and under her orange jersey she has small beginnings of breasts. Watching her skate so effortlessly among a hundred other skaters, I almost don't recognize her.

As she makes the circuit without me, I push myself clumsily forward on scuffed, brown skates that seem too big, too loose. There is a smell of new paint mingled with old dust. The old brown paint on the walls shows through the thin new coat of yellow.

"Let's race," she says and zips past me, not even waiting for me to agree. Off she goes, weaving skillfully between slower, more leisurely skaters. I try to follow her but lose my balance and grab the railing.

"Where were you?" she says, dragging the toe of her right skate and slowing down next to me. She continues to skate in little circles as we talk. She's smiling, but it's not Peggy behind the smile. Her cheeks are thinner, like some older girl, like some young woman.

"You could have waited for me," I say.

"It's a race. You don't wait."

Two boys about my age go thundering past us, elbowing each other playfully, weaving and dodging around other skaters.

"All right," I say. "You want to race? OK, let's do it."

I push off from the railing, but Peggy is already ten yards ahead and not looking back. Now I'm mad that she is so much faster and better, and I say, "Dammit!" and try to kick the railing. Big mistake. I am flat on my back, and my right elbow hurts so much it's partially numb. The two boys who just raced past us nearly pile into me. They manage to jump over me and crouch into perfect eight-wheel landings.

"Jack, are you OK?" Peggy says, completing her third circuit as I struggle to an upright position.

"Yeah. But it hurts like hell."

Peggy looks at the skinned and bleeding elbow. "Shit, Dad will be mad at me. You'll have to get a Band-Aid on it."

"I don't happen to carry one with me, do you?"

"Don't get smart. Just go wash it off in the boys' room."

I start to unlace my skates.

"What are you doing?"

"I can't skate in the men's room, can I? Anyway, I don't even feel like skating."

Peggy lets her breath out and looks out at the kaleidoscope of skaters. Late afternoon sun slices through a high window. I turn toward the sunlight, but a cloud passes in front of it. I sit on the bench and unlace my skates. Peggy sits next to me, every so often looking up at the skaters going around and around.

The sunlight reappears. Tiny white motes of dust drift aimlessly in and out of the beam. "Hey," I say. "The whites are back."

"What?"

"The whites. We used to play Clap the Whites."

"Oh. Right." She reaches into the sunlight and claps her hands. The dust motes swarm, panic-stricken. I reach in and clap.

"Got one!" I say.

Peggy starts to laugh and cuts off the sound. I say, "This is where you say, 'Did not!' and I say, 'Did too!' Remember?"

Peggy sighs again and looks out at the skaters. Without a word, she slips under the railing and merges with the whirling mass. I watch as she vanishes into the crowd, then my eye goes back to the dust motes that have slowed to a lazy, aimless hovering. I focus on the brightest one, and it seems to drift toward me. I reach for it, and it vanishes into the shadows.

26

Mother Remigius discovers early that it is easy to get Jack Sheedy to cry in front of the fourth grade class. Sister Josita, the four-foot nun who taught me in third grade, must have tipped her off. Was it because I, the shortest boy in the class, was somehow a threat to Josita's own shortness? A mockery? A challenge? A deliberate insult? Was that why, when I failed to recite the seven table perfectly, she resorted to the ruler slap? Or, even worse, the red marking pencil on the top of my head?

I thought that graduating from Josita to Remigius would be a reprieve. After all, Remigius liked me enough to personally bathe me when I was delivered to her after the flood. During the first days of school following the flood, Mother Remigius would tell the class the story of how the Sheedys survived in the attic, rescued the Houghs, lost their possessions, and were guests of the Sisters of Saint Joseph and Father Byrne for three days—carefully leaving out any mention of The Bath.

But then the bloom left the rose, and I still struggle to understand how it happened. I have memorized everything but the eleven and twelve tables, so that can't be it. I am two whole tables ahead of most of the class. My spelling, grammar, reading and composition are ahead of all but one or two others. Whatever I am supposed to learn about myself from Mother Remigius's incessant ridicule, I must never have learned.

"Stand up!" she yells at me one day. And when I do, she recites a list of what I must have done or said wrong. It feels impertinent of me to be attempting to tell this episode, when all I remember of it is the humiliation. I am a prisoner in the dock, and a judge in black robes is listing my crimes, but all I hear in my memory is my own whimpering.

"Stop sniveling! You will be staying after school if you don't stop right now!"

It's no use. The more she scolds, the more the tears fall. I look around to see which kids are gawking at the crybaby. All the girls are staring at their hands folded on the desk. The boys are looking out windows or pretending to read. Still, these are the kids I must face at recess.

Mother Remigius follows me to fifth grade, and then to sixth. She sends home report cards with C's, D's, and F's. I am a loner in the schoolyard, only occasionally hanging around with one or two other boys. At home, I wet the bed nearly every night.

In the schoolyard, I swing high on the swings, singing, "You touch my hand and what a thrill I got, your lips are like a volcano that's hot." Mother Frigidaire is staring at me from the school steps. Back inside, she lectures the class against singing Elvis Presley songs on school property. She doesn't look at me, but everyone else does. I feel all shook up for days.

It doesn't seem to matter whether I study or not. I still get C's and D's. Maybe Dad's wrong. Maybe I'm not that smart. Maybe I'm actually dumb.

I try hard to learn to play baseball well in that schoolyard, but it's useless. Pitchers always walk halfway to the plate, lob the ball to me underhand, and still strike me out on three pitches. In the outfield, I can't catch the easiest popup. Then one day I walk onto the field just as Ralph Parent hits one toward the third base pine tree. It bounces from limb to limb and falls into my second-hand first baseman's glove.

At Saint Mary's School, there seems to be no correlation between attempt and result.

In the fall of 1958, in seventh grade, Mother Remigius is gone. Sister Mary Jane is my new teacher. Mom schedules an appointment with her to try to understand why my marks have been so low the past three years. Sister Mary Jane swings open her black ledger and sees nothing but A's and B's after my name. Mother Remigius had been keeping two sets of books on me. One for the Archdiocese. One for me.

Put it behind you, people say. OK, but how do I get back those three years? How do I change my bad opinions of myself now? Let's say you're running a marathon and the timekeeper has it in for you. You run your heart out, but your time is only three hours. Fair, but nothing spectacular. So you unlace your running shoes and decide to try a different career. Years later, you discover the time was recorded wrong. It was really two hours. A world record! How many boxes of Wheaties could you have been on?

After Mother Remigius leaves, I stop wetting the bed. And, even though Sister Mary Jane occasionally scolds me, I never cry.

The only other change is that Peggy has just graduated from eighth grade and now attends Regional 7 High School. I am the oldest Sheedy in Saint Mary's. Oh, and the girls sitting next to me look different. Protruding under their blue-and-white Saint Mary's School uniforms are perky little breasts that inspire distracting physiological changes in me.

In eighth grade, I fall in love with Kathy Kavanaugh. In the Secret Santa drawing, Richie Bouchard draws her name, and I pay him a dollar for it. That gives me the right to buy her a present for the 1959 Christmas party. So I buy her a box of candy, wrap it up with a pink bow, bring it to the party, all nervous.

Kathy doesn't show.

Her parents have transferred her to the junior high section of Regional 7. Top it all off, I have to draw another name: Richie Bouchard. He gets my dollar, and he gets a four-dollar tin of Schrafft's candy to boot.

Peggy teases me. "Your girlfriend goes to my school now."

"She's not my girlfriend."

"But you like her. And you were supposed to buy her a present."

"How do you know?"

"Everybody knows."

She laughs and goes to her room. I wander from room to room. Mom is watching Jack Benny and assembling a jigsaw puzzle of men scaling a mountain. The television script is about a rehearsal for the Jack Benny Show, something that never really becomes a show. The snow-clad mountain in the puzzle is impossibly high, but the faces on the climbers look hopeful; still, the moment is frozen in time, broken in pieces.

27

Mom never gets to sit down to eat with us. She puts the pork roast on the table for Dad to slice and then dollops the mashed potatoes into a serving bowl and sets it on the countertop. Dad takes two serving spoonfuls and passes the bowl to Peggy. She takes a scoop, passes it down the line to Ann, Tom, Gerald, and finally me. Then Mom leads us in a quick "Bless us O Lord and these thy gifts which we are about to receive from thy bounty through Christ our Lord Amen" and everybody digs in. Except Mom. She's back at the stove, getting the string beans.

This is not a traditional dinner table. After the flood, the remodeled kitchen features a D-shaped snack bar. Mom and Dad sit at the top of the curve. I sit at the bottom, and all the serving bowls accumulate in front of me.

Now Mom is getting the milk bottle out, shaking it up to mix the cream, and pouring glasses for the five kids. Peggy is asking Dad for more pork. Tom reaches across Gerald's plate to get a second helping of the mashed potatoes that are still in front of me. Mom has to open a second quart of Burdick's Dairy milk, and the cardboard cap collapses and falls into the bottle. Dad finally gets up to help find which cabinet drawer they keep the extra milk bottle caps for just such an emergency, and Ann is asking for more string beans.

Dad tweezes the soggy cap from inside the milk bottle and pours another glass for Gerald. Mom tells Dad to sit down because there isn't room for two in the tiny kitchen space. "Yuck, it's all queam!" Gerald says, and Mom says, "Oh *dear*, I forgot to shake it!" Dad says, "No, it's my fault." Mom takes back Gerald's glass and Peggy warns her, "Don't pour it back, he already drank out of it!" I am still waiting for my first glass of milk as Mom finds a faux crystal pitcher and fills it with Gerald's cream. She shakes up the just-opened bottle, pours milk into Gerald's glass, then adds just a bit more cream from the pitcher. "I'll keep the pitcher for my coffee," she says. Then she sits down.

"I thought there was gravy," Ann says, and Mom pops up again.

"Could you grab me another Miller?" Dad says.

"I didn't get any milk," I say.

"I'm finished," Tom announces. "Is there any dessert?"

Mom overfills the gravy boat and it flows onto the Formica countertop. "Oh *dear!*" she yells. "Jack, I mean Gerald, I mean Tom, can't you just wait? I haven't even sat down yet!"

"My be scused?" Gerald asks.

"No, you will sit right there until everyone is finished," Mom says. "I haven't even poured myself a glass of water."

"All right, listen," Dad says, placing his napkin on the table. He reminds me of Robert Young from "Father Knows Best." "Here are the new rules. No one begins eating until all the food is served. Then we say grace. When your mother sits down and takes her first bite, then the meal begins."

Peggy is enthusiastic about the idea, and that's good enough for the rest of us. The new system goes into effect the very next evening, and it works pretty smoothly. The evening after that, we are still having fun with it. After "Christ our Lord Amen," the five kids each hold a forkful of chicken in front of our open mouths and stare at Mom as she wipes the counter, sits down and spreads her napkin on her lap. She glances around at us, smiles uneasily and takes a quick bite. We all dig in like ravenous hogs, and Mom gets up to pour herself a glass of water and put the apple pie on a trivet so it will be cool enough to slice for dessert. Tom asks her for an extra napkin.

Mom still finishes last, and the rules are modified. No one may be excused until everyone is finished.

This works fine until Ann's petit mal seizures begin.

"Why don't you pay attention?" Peggy frowns at Ann one night.

"What? I am," Ann says.

"Were you praying?"

"No. We already said grace. I was eating."

"You were staring at your plate. Your whole body was rocking."

"I was not. I asked for the spinach. Then I looked up and saw it was already in front of me, along with the rice."

"That's because you weren't paying attention. We passed you the spinach, then Tom asked for the rice. You wouldn't pass it along."

The next night, Mom notices it too. Ann is bringing a forkful of peas to her mouth and freezes. The peas spill back onto her plate. Ann's eyes are open but she's not with us. Her upper body moves back and forth, her head getting lower and lower. Mom calls her name. She doesn't respond. Thirty seconds later, Ann blinks, straightens up and takes another forkful of peas, as though no time had elapsed.

Dr. Markwald says it's a form of epilepsy, probably a result of a high fever when she had measles. He sends her to a neurologist in Hartford, who puts her on Mysoline. "I still think she was just trying to get attention," Peggy says to me as she hands me a dish to dry. "She's always doing weird stuff to get attention."

"Like what?" I say, even though I already agree.

"Like whispering to herself in her room," Peggy says. "And answering herself."

"I know. Sometimes I try to listen outside her door, but I can't figure out what they're saying. I mean what *she's* saying."

"I think she doesn't have epilepsy at all. She's faking. She wants to keep everybody at the table until she's finished, and it's all intentional."

Except that the Mysoline is working. After the dosage is figured out, the episodes diminish, and Ann finishes eating about the same time everyone else does.

Peggy chooses to ignore this. Instead, she finds a printout of Ann's electroencephalogram and pretends to be the technician who analyzes it. Peggy and I sit by ourselves at the kitchen counter giggling over the seismic spikes on the long spool of graph paper. "Ah, ziss iss not goot!" Peggy says, and marks a big spike with a pencil. "Ziss clearly shows lunatic tendencies. Do you see, Herr Doctor?"

"Uh, yes I quite concur," I say.

"So, ve vill haff to conclude she iss a maniac!" Peggy says, writing "MANIAC!!!" in large capital letters on the EEG.

"A sad case," I say.

"Ah, quite so," she says. "Verrry, verrry sad," and we giggle until we can hardly breathe.

28

Bruce Baxter joins Boy Scouts a few months after I do, in the winter of 1957-58. His khaki brown uniform looks great on him, crisply ironed by his mom. The brass belt buckle shines as if newly polished, and the red neckerchief is fluffed slightly as it emerges from the metal slide. My own uniform feels limp, the trouser legs a bit long, with Mom's assurance that I'll "grow into them."

We sit in the back of the room at Scout meetings, giggling at the vaguely phallic pictures of half-hitches and bowlines in our manuals, until Dick Markwald—Dr. Markwald's son, an assistant scoutmaster—yells at us to "Keep it to a dull roar."

That expression makes us laugh out loud for some reason. Bad idea.

"OK, you two. Atten-hut!" And he stiffens and gives the three-finger Boy Scout salute. Bruce and I jump to our feet and salute in return.

"Wipe those smiles off your faces!"

We try to look serious.

"Did you HEAR me?"

"Yes!" we say in unison.

"Yes, what?"

"Yes, sir!"

"Then do it—like this!" And Dick Markwald grins and rubs his hand across his mouth. When his hand leaves his face, the grin is a scowl. "Do it now!"

Bruce and I wipe the smiles off our faces.

"Troop thirty-nine, form a paddling mill, on the double! Sheedy and Baxter, stay at attention."

Twelve boys form two facing rows. Richie Bouchard and John McGurk are rubbing their hands together and smirking.

"You smirk, you're next," Dick warns.

The smirks are gone.

"Baxter, front and center. NOW!"

Bruce approaches the double line of Scouts.

"Is the mill ready?"

"Yes, sir!" the twelve boys shout.

"Baxter—GO!"

Bruce runs quickly between the rows of Scouts, trying to avoid the butt-spankings each one tries to administer. Nevertheless, he gets at least eight hits and barrels full speed into the wall of the New Hartford Fire Department's basement. He turns toward the Scouts and salutes dutifully.

"Tuck that shirt in!" Dick orders.

Bruce adjusts his uniform, and he looks as natty as ever, none the worse for wear.

"Sheedy!"

"Yes, sir!"

"Don't yes-sir me, you know the drill. Front and center, and GO!"

I take a ten-foot running start and fly through the mill, barely getting three direct spankings. I stop well short of the wall, swivel and salute. The Scouts are applauding my dodging abilities, some are laughing, and perversely I respond by smiling and bowing like an actor at curtain call.

Bad idea number two.

Dick Markwald puts two fingers to his mouth and lets out the shrillest whistle I ever heard. In the silence it commands, we can hear water dripping from a lavatory somewhere. Dick, ramrod tall, marches over to me, bends down and nearly touches his nose to mine. His command is barely audible: "Again."

"Sir?"

He straightens. "I said again, Sheedy."

"Yes, sir."

I walk to the front of the mill and lean forward, like a sprinter at his mark.

"At my command," Dick says.

"Yes, sir."

"On your mark. Get set. Oh, and by the way, Sheedy?"

I glance up at him. "Sir?"

"Listen carefully to my command. Back on your mark. Get set."

The moment lasts forever. Finally the command comes:

"Sheedy, walk."

The faces of the Scouts in the mill are terrified, like members of a firing squad who have lifted the blindfold from their victim, seeing the terror reflected in his eyes. I take one step, and Tim Krom pretends to wallop me, making a loud contact but not following through. That one doesn't hurt. Opposite Tim, Travers Auburn nods gravely at me, then rears back and lets his big right arm swing through. But he keeps his hand loose and lets it glance off the side of my butt, causing only a little sting. And so on through the line, each boy trying to make the spanking look good, each one holding back just a bit. Finally, John McGurk and Richie Bouchard. John may be thinking that he has to do what is expected, so he gives a little sorry-about-that headshake and wallops my ass until I nearly hit the concrete. Richie grins, sees it's OK to let loose, and cuffs my butt like he's volleying a handball, and I am propelled into the wall, bounce off and land on the concrete floor. My knee is like hamburger, and my uniform trousers are torn at the knee.

I struggle to my feet and salute.

"At ease, Sheedy."

Feet apart, hands clasped behind me.

"Troop, fall out. Back to your seats."

But I stay where I am.

"Dick?" I say.

Dick's eyebrow goes up. "What did you call me?"

"Sorry. Richard, I mean."

"Don't mock me, Sheedy. I can drum you right out of—"

"Dick, can we stop the army stuff for a minute?"

Dick opens his mouth but nothing comes out.

"I mean, it's just us," I continue. "Your dad's my doctor, my mom's your school nurse, John's dad's our resident trooper."

He tries to interrupt, but he doesn't know what to say. His mouth opens and shuts like a fish.

I don't know what to do with the silence. "I mean, we're just a bunch of guys here," I finally continue. "Kids from the same town, same school some of us. Tim and I play ice hockey together. Eddy and I play football at his house. And you made me rip my pants."

All this would be very eloquent and like a Frank Capra movie speech by Jimmy Stewart, except I am bawling my eyes out by now and kids are hanging their heads, embarrassed for me. Dick rubs his chin and clears his throat.

"All right, troop! Team up, one on one, test each other on, uh, Morse Code for ten minutes. Sheedy—uh, Jack—follow me."

We walk out into the dark March night, where islands of snow reflect streetlamps. It is raining, and we stand under the overhang of the roof, shove our hands in our pockets.

"Look," Dick says. "Mr. Sheffield's not here. He put me in charge, OK? I'm trying, doing my best. I'm sorry about the pants."

"It's OK, Mom'll sew them."

"Let me see."

Dick has brought an Army-green, official Boy Scout flashlight, and he shines it on my torn trousers. It's not just a tear, it's a right-angle tear, a corner peeled away. The kind of tear that needs a patch. Underneath, my knee is still bleeding.

"Hurt?"

"Yeah. Stings."

"Well, let's at least get you some first aid. Come on in and—"

"I'll do it," a voice says.

"Who's there? Who said that?" Dick shines the flashlight in the direction of the voice.

Bruce is standing in the rain fifteen feet away, water dripping off his Boy Scout cap and onto his epaulets.

"I'll do it," Bruce says. "It was my fault."

Bruce and I go inside, climb to an upstairs room, and Dick follows with a first aid kit. "This will be for your Second Class badge," Dick says to Bruce. "I have to witness."

"You don't have to do this," I tell Bruce, sliding the braided belt out of the brass buckle and removing my trousers.

"It's all right," he says. "It's just that it's my fault we were laughing in the first place."

He washes the knee with a cold wet cloth, and it hurts like hell. I try not to react, but I let out a quick "Ow! Shit!"

"Hey! Language!" Dick says.

"Sorry. I meant 'Shoot!'" I say, and even Dick laughs now.

Bruce rinses the cloth in a basin of water, wrings it out, and presses it to my knee for a minute until he's sure the bleeding's stopped. Then he takes the dreaded iodine bottle, drenches a ball of cotton, and says, "Ready?"

I just take a deep breath.

Days later, Tim Krom will tell me that my scream from upstairs made him completely forget whether the letter R is dot-dash-dot or dash-dot-dash.

"OK, you're good," Bruce says when he finishes wrapping the bandage. "I guess you should change it before you go to bed, case it bleeds through."

"Thanks, Bruce. I owe you, I guess."

Dick shakes his head, smiles. "You two are something. All right, Jack, get dressed. God knows what they all think we're doing up here."

That night, Mom admires the bandage Bruce made, but she's upset about the pants. "I just bought these new at Colt's in Winsted," she says.

"They made me go through the mill," I say.

"The what?"

I tell her the whole story. Mom calls Dr. Markwald. That weekend, she drives me to Colt's and has me try on a new pair of pants. "Perfect," she says. "You'll grow into them."

"I didn't last time, did I?" I say. "Shorten them an inch."

The man with the tape measure nods at Mom, takes back the pants, shortens them, wraps them up. Mom fishes in her purse. "That won't be necessary," the man says. "Dr. Markwald has taken care of it."

29

There are times when I think Dad will leave home forever. "There once was a man who went to mail a letter," he likes to tell us. "He never returned." He repeats this so often that I expect him to disappear each time he raises the red flag on our mailbox. But he always returns.

There is one close call in 1958, after an argument with Mom about money, or rather about the lack of it, and the first thing I know, Dad is packing his tan Samsonite and throwing it into the trunk of our 1956 blue-and-white Chevy V-eight. "He'll be back," Mom says softly, her eyes focused on the green flecked pattern of the Formica kitchen countertop.

She is right, but Dad doesn't return for several days. It is while I am reading a Superman comic for the seventh time, an episode where Clark Kent is feeling deathly ill and no one can figure out why. When I get to the part where he realizes he's been exposed to kryptonite, I hear the car door slam. I look out my bedroom window and see Dad trudging solemnly in, carrying the Samsonite. I know Mom is in the kitchen that Dad must walk through, but from my room I can't see them. I tiptoe out to the upstairs landing and hear the kitchen floor creak under Dad's heavy footsteps. There is a brief silence and then the footsteps start up again. Now I see Dad at the bottom of the stairs, lugging his baggage, and I duck back out of sight.

The next day, he takes his five kids out for ice cream and tells us a daydream.

"Once upon a time," he says, "a cowboy left the ranch because he was tired and poor and ashamed that he had nothing to give. He traveled alone, following the sun for a few days, and slept under the stars with his trusty horse who always knew the way. But the cowboy missed his home and family, and a few days later, he turned his back to the sun and spurred his steed on toward home, where he kissed his wife and hugged his children and lived happily ever after. Now, who wants chocolate ice cream?"

A year and a few months later, in early December 1959, Dad announces he is going to drive to California in a 1960 Thunderbird. "I saw this classified ad in *The Hartford Courant*," he tells us. "Gengras Motors of Hartford wants someone to drive a brand new T-Bird to another Ford dealer in Los Angeles. I'll be home for Christmas."

Mom stares at the squiggly pattern on the Toastmaster toaster. Peggy and I gaze blankly up at Dad's face, which continues to smile. Ann, Tom and Gerald protest, beg him to stay. "They're paying me to do this!" he says. "I wish everyone could come with me, but they won't allow it."

He leaves three days later, mailing postcards from all his stops: Palisades Park, New Jersey; Washington, D.C.; Bethune, South Carolina; Columbus, Georgia; Brewton, Alabama; New Orleans; Hockley, Fredericksburg and Bakersfield, Texas; Las Cruces, New Mexico; and finally Los Angeles. "This car is a cream puff," one card says. "Better highway ahead. Feeling fine. Shirtsleeves most of the way. Seems like Xmas in springtime. Wish I had taken one of the children. I'll be home for Xmas. Love John."

But it begins to look as if he won't make it home for Christmas, because he is enjoying his visit with his sister, my Aunt Julia, and her family. He is not home for me to confide in about my humiliation over Kathy Kavanaugh and the Secret Santa. I bottle myself in my bedroom, scribbling "I love Kathy!" over and over again in my diary. I can't think of anything else, except that Dad's not here.

There is no reason why a man would leave his family two weeks before Christmas, to drive, alone, across a whole continent. Three times in his postcards he writes, "Wish I had taken one of the children." But he didn't. And it would probably have been Peggy anyway. She is his darling, a black-haired, hazel-eyed, elfin beauty, who has no time in her life for me anymore. Peggy has her girlfriends who squeal over Elvis records, and she has her boyfriends, whom I don't even want to think about. There are strange boys, big, tall, muscular, hormonal boys who drool over her and dance the bop with her. She is everyone else's sweetheart.

Dad flies home on TWA the day before Christmas Eve. He is filled with stories about acres of cotton fields in Georgia, bright lights and sweet music in New Orleans, a never-ending state of Texas that he vowed he would cross in a day. He tells about infinite desert highways in Arizona, where distant mountains kept receding as he approached them. He tells of meeting a tractor trailer in the middle of the desert, and how when the driver blinked his headlights in greeting, Dad cried in sheer loneliness.

He had no business leaving home.

That night, when everyone is in bed, I listen at the top of the stairs to Mom's whispered voice talking to Dad: "...paid a dollar for her name, and the day of the party he finds out she was transferred to Regional."

There is a two-second silence, then a muffled clap of Dad's hand on his knee, followed by his quick burst of laughter, quickly stifled. My face is hot, but I don't cry. I cradle my rosary in the cup of my hand and Hail Mary myself to sleep.

30

Bruce wants to start a club, with him and me as the only members. He builds a tarpaper-covered clubhouse in his backyard, and we meet there sometimes. Other times, we meet in the clubhouse Eddy Allen and I built a year or two earlier, down behind the ruins of the Lyn Gas building. Both clubhouses were built with scrap lumber from Lyn Gas.

Other times, we get together with Gil Coan and play whiffle ball. Gil usually wins. Or we get together with Eddy Allen and play football. Eddy wins.

In January 1960, Bruce and I go sledding on Shepard's Hill. He leaves early, says he has a sore throat.

His parents take him to Dr. Markwald, who puts him in the hospital. Swollen glands, is what we hear. Early in February, as Mom is driving me to Scouts, she says, "I have some bad news. Mrs. Baxter told me that Bruce may have either leukemia or cancer of the lymph glands. He doesn't know it yet."

"Cancer? Is he going to be all right?"

"No. If he has leukemia, he might live a year or two. If he has lymph gland cancer, he'll live longer, maybe ten years."

Two weeks later, there is a Scout patrol meeting at Bruce's house, and Tim Krom and John McGurk are there. Bruce looks pale, but he seems cheerful, reads some jokes from *Boys' Life* magazine. By now, the diagnosis is confirmed: leukemia. Tim and John and I know, but we don't talk about it.

I don't entirely avoid Bruce, but I don't know how to talk to him. He must know he's dying by now, but how do you talk about that? And how do you ignore it?

One Saturday morning, I see Bruce across the strawberry patch, coming outside to feed his dog, Bessie. I wave to him, and he waves back. Weeks earlier, I would have crossed over and sat down with him on the cement steps that Mr. Bills made as a finishing touch to the house about seven or eight years ago. Now, I just wave. Bruce waves back, and I look away first. I look up again in time to see him disappear through the kitchen door.

I know the layout of his house perfectly from when only the skeleton timbers framed its shape. I imagine him walking into the kitchen, saying something to his mother. She maybe gives him a hug, tells him to rest, get his strength back. He walks into the dining room, turns right and goes into the living room, then turns again and walks up the stairs, stepping on the tread where I bent a nail trying to help Mr. Bills nine years ago. I picture him walking left at the landing, going down a narrow hallway to his room on the north side of the house, facing the bedroom I share with my brothers on this side of the strawberry field. I recall that just weeks ago Bruce and I would practice Morse Code with flashlights between the two windows. There would be confusion because both of us would use the flashlight to look up the code in the Boy Scout manual, and we would both mistake each other's flickering lights for signaling. "What does 'LKYKZX' mean?" I would ask the next day, and we would collapse in laughter.

I am still watching Baxters' house when I remember this, and I see the shade in Bruce's room lower all the way. It comes back up just a couple inches. I pretend I don't see it.

For my fourteenth birthday, Mom and Dad give me a blue Explorer uniform, which only a couple other Scouts in our troop are old enough to wear. When the man at Colt's shortens them to a half-inch longer than my ideal length, he winks at me. "I'm betting you'll wear these until you use that half-inch," he says.

In the spring, I graduate from Saint Mary's School and am looking forward to freshman year at Regional 7 High School, where I will again see my beloved Kathy Kavanaugh. I have little time for Boy Scouts, because the summer is taken up with my first foray into journalism, the writing and publication of a family-based newspaper I call *The New Hartford Frontier Register*.

The name is inspired by Democratic candidate John F. Kennedy's "New Frontier" speech. I use Dad's Thermofax copying machine to reproduce the weekly, typewritten gossip sheet, and I lend copies of it to neighbors, including the Millers and the Baxters. Ann writes a column about British royalty. Peggy draws pictures and designs advertisements. Tom helps with the copying. Gerald writes and draws a couple of original comic strips. Dad and Mom contribute jokes and gossip. I even get unsolicited columns from townspeople.

Dad finances the paper, which loses money—about twenty dollars in materials. Mr. Grinvalsky, owner of the Marble Pharmacy, offers to sell the paper in his store, and *Hartford Courant* reporter Joe O'Brien calls me for an interview. "14-year-old is publisher of new paper," his story is headlined. I bask in fame all summer, all the time hoping that the girl I love will call and tell me how wonderful the newspaper is.

She doesn't, and I sing along with the Everly Brothers a lot that summer. I'm Kathy's clown. I see her in church, sitting with her family near the front, and I can't take my eyes off her. She is about my height, has dark hair, dark eyes, a slight overbite that seems charming, and horn-rimmed glasses that I think make her look intelligent. No one is preventing me from talking to her, but I have no idea how to start. Maybe she would shun me, scold me, tell all her friends that Jack Sheedy is a conceited snob for daring to talk to her. It's safer to do nothing. I'll just do nothing, and that way I can think about her and imagine us somehow thrown together in a room, alone, so that we would *have* to talk to one another, and she would *have* to like me. I imagine buying flowers for her and walking to her house in Pine Meadow and ringing the doorbell of her steep-roofed, black-and-red house, being ushered in by her smiling parents, and sitting with her on the sofa, where we would smile at each other and maybe even talk. It's the talking part that's hardest to imagine. There might not be anything to talk about. Maybe I would say, "Don't you hope Kennedy gets elected?" And what would she say? "Kennedy! Don't you like Nixon?" And that would be the end of our conversation and our love.

Now I sing another Everly Brothers song, just as appropriate. I'm dreaming my life away.

Peggy is always away somewhere. She goes to slumber parties at her friend Lee's house, or she gets driven to see movies at The Strand in Winsted. Mom gives her permission to see movies with boys if it's a double date. She doesn't give permission to see "Butterfield 8," which *The Catholic Transcript* lists as one of the Legion of Decency's condemned movies, but Peggy sees it anyway, because people say she looks like Elizabeth Taylor.

One day, I catch Peggy practicing the jitterbug by herself in the living room, to one of her Elvis forty-fives. She has a bottle of Coke in one hand. There are three empty Coke bottles on the lamp stand near the record player. She sees me and stops, takes a swig, lifts the needle off the record, and the room fills with silence. "Well?" she says. I turn to go. "All right, wait," she says. "I'll teach you to jitterbug."

I look at her, wondering how to react.

"Don't you want to learn?" she says. "So you can dance with Kathy?"

"I'll never dance with Kathy. How come you're drinking all the Coke?"

"I'm thirsty. And you won't dance with Kathy if you don't learn how. OK, pay attention."

She shows me how to stand while the girl is spinning, how not to get my wrists twisted when we're doing that back-to-back twirl while holding hands, how to push the girl back and pull the girl closer to me, push her back, pull her closer, then twirl her around like a top with my upraised arm. At least that's what she tries to show me. My legs aren't listening, my arms aren't remembering, and my knees and elbows are bumping into her.

"All right, never mind for now. Hey, I can show you some easy ones, like the bunny hop. And you have to learn how to waltz. That's the one you'll really want to dance with Kathy."

The bunny hop is stupid, but easy. The waltz is embarrassing, especially with my sister. I don't know how to react. This is Peggy, but we're not playing with ants in the driveway anymore, or helping Mr. Bills build the skeleton house. She's a beautiful fifteen-year-old girl with a perfectly shaped body. I'm waltzing with her, close together, my right hand on her back, left hand holding her right. Her left hand rests on my shoulder. She pushes me a few inches from her, so there is no other contact. We dance to "Love Me Tender." As Elvis finishes up with, "…and I always will," I'm actually not thinking about Kathy.

"That was OK," she says. "At least you can waltz. Now do you want to know why I wanted you to learn?"

"So you could practice, right? Because you have a date." I am probably pouting.

"Don't be a jerk. I don't have a date. But I am going to the dance in Winsted on Saturday."

"Alone?"

"Girls don't go to dances alone. Unless they're, you know. Sluts."

"So how can you go, if you don't have a date?"

"I wanted Lee to go, but she can't. So I talked to Dad, and he said it would be OK to go with somebody else."

"Who?"

"You."

"What? I don't think so."

"But dancing is fun. And all you ever do is mope around in your room, writing in your diary or staring at the ceiling for hours."

"But I can't date my sister."

"You'd rather write 'I love Kathy' in your diary all the time?"

I glare at her. "How much did you read?"

She sips her Coke. "I didn't read anything. I just guessed."

"You lie. How do you even know I have a diary? I keep it in my desk."

"You just admitted it."

"You just admitted you read it."

"No. I just know how you are. You're holed up in your room too much."

"Because there's nothing to do." I want to add, *because you're always gone*, but I don't.

"You can play with Tom and Gerald," she says.

"All they talk about is cars. I don't like cars."

"Or Ann."

"She's always reading about kings and queens. Dad's always working, and Mom's always doing her puzzles or playing solitaire or knitting or watching TV. It's boring here."

"So that's settles it."

"What?"

"We'll go dancing. Peggy and Jack. Saturday night."

She guzzles the last of her Coke.

"Why am I always so thirsty?" she asks.

31

Mom drops Peggy and me off at the Hinsdale School gymnasium. Inside, there are yellow and red balloons and streamers. The bleachers are painted battleship gray and smell like old sneakers. Peggy is wearing a white dress with a red carnation corsage. I am wearing my blue Confirmation suit. I am actually excited about the dance, because I'm with a pretty girl and nobody has to know she's my sister.

The man takes our ticket money and tears off our ticket stubs. His name tag says "MR. O'MALLEY." He grins down at me. "So lookit the two of you. If it isn't your own sister you're bringin to the dance!"

Peggy and I stare at each other. She bursts out laughing. The man is still grinning.

"Do you know us?" I manage to squeak.

"Not a-tall. But have you seen yourselves? Is it twins you are?"

"Almost," Peggy says.

Mr. O'Malley's forehead forms great furrows. "Almost twins? Would you be explainin that?"

"When I was maybe six weeks old, Mom and Dad drove me to Danvers, Massachusetts," Peggy says. "To show me off to my grandparents. Dad and Mom slept in Dad's old bedroom. Dad had the bright idea to start a new baby right there, in his old bedroom. So that's what they did."

112

Mr. O'Malley is looking away and rubbing various parts of his face. "Well," he says, "there's a bit more detail than I expected. Never mind! Off with you. Enjoy the dance!"

Peggy is giggling into her fist as she leads me toward the refreshment table. "How was that for getting him to shut up?" she says.

"Pretty quick thinking. You're better than Dad at making up stories."

"Who's making up stories? Mom told me that. And you know Mom. She can't tell a lie if it came with instructions."

"You mean they—"

"She didn't want to. Not yet. But yeah. Now buy me a Coke."

I buy two Cokes in Dixie Cups. Peggy drinks hers in a gulp, then eyeballs mine. I give it to her and buy myself another one. "Hey, these are fifteen cents a cup," I say. "That's not cheap."

"I can't help it if I'm thirsty."

The band starts playing the Mexican Hat Dance.

"Here we go!" Peggy says.

"But you didn't teach me this one!"

"Oh, just watch. It's easy."

Easy and idiotic, I think. *Hands on hips, hats on floor. Da-dump, da-dump, da-dump.*

"I'll be right back. I have to pee," Peggy says after the last "Olé!"

"Again?"

"Maybe you can find some girl to dance with."

"Maybe you shouldn't drink so much Coke."

While she's gone I sit in the bleachers and watch couples dance the jitterbug and know I can never do it. Then I watch them waltz, and I know I could never ask a girl to dance that way. Then I watch the same couples dance to "The Twist," and I start to think that I could maybe manage that one. If only all the girls weren't already taken.

Of course, if Peggy would get out of the girls' room before the last "round and around and around," I could twist with her.

"Have ye got a dime on ye, lad?"

It's Mr. O'Malley, his face red and beaded with sweat from running across the floor to find me.

"What? Uh, yeah."

"Call your home then and tell your parents to come get the both of ye."

"What? Did we do something?"

"It's your sister. She's lookin a mite poorly, lad."

32

Two days later, Mom hands Peggy a Sunkist orange and a syringe. "Remember, tap the syringe with your fingernail, like this," Mom says. "Get the air bubbles out."

I'm sitting in the den, right off the kitchen where Mom and Peggy are, and they don't see me.

"It's a good thing you're a nurse," Peggy says, her eyes bright with tears.

"Just tap the syringe. That's good. Now rub the alcohol-soaked cotton on the orange and inject it at an angle."

Peggy stabs the orange.

"That's good. But more of an angle. That would go too deep in your own arm."

Peggy buries her face in her hands. "I don't want to have to do this!" she says.

"You'll have to do it, sweetheart. You'll have to do it every day of your life now."

"I thought I was just thirsty because it's summer and it's hot. Then I had to pee all the time, and I was hungry all the time, and I got tired all of a sudden."

"That Mr. O'Malley said you had your face under the faucet in the ladies' room for a long time and another girl was worried and told him. You couldn't get enough water to quench your thirst."

"Maybe I'll get over it. You know? Grow out of it or something."

"There is no cure. Your Aunt Anna has this, too. It's in the family. It often shows up in the teenage years," Mom says.

That night, Mom and Dad gather the family together to tell us about Peggy's disease. For once, Mom does all the talking, and Dad listens with his head down. "She can't eat a lot of sugar," Mom says, discussing Peggy as though she weren't sitting right there with her head in her hands. "And she has to have a needle every day. She has to keep finding new places on her body to inject herself. And once she injects herself, she has to make sure she eats something or she'll go into a coma. She can also go into a different kind of coma if she eats too much, especially too much sugar. Otherwise, she can lead a normal life."

Nobody talks. Nobody asks questions. Later, Peggy, Mom and Dad lock themselves in Peggy's bedroom and talk, while Ann, Tom, Gerald and I watch "Perry Mason." Ann stares unblinking at the TV. Tom and Gerald poke each other and argue over the easy chair. Then they settle down, all their squabbling energy drained. Perry Mason wins as usual, but this time it is close.

On weekends, Peggy mopes around in bathrobe and slippers, drinking water, eating salads, not saying much to anyone. We meet on the stairs and don't make eye contact. I think about how horrible it must be not to be able to eat Mom's apple pie. How Peggy must dread every morning when she has to deliberately stab herself with a sharp needle. How she has to think all the time about what she eats, how much she eats, when she can eat, and all those desserts she can never eat.

A long, quiet week later, I hear Elvis singing from the living room phonograph, asking to be treated like a fool. Peggy is dancing with a broom. A glass of water and a half-eaten carrot are on the lamp stand. Elvis is saying he would beg and steal. Peggy glances over her shoulder, smiles, already knowing I have sneaked in on her.

"I'm going to be OK, you know," she says.

"I know. I mean, I hope so," I say.

"I mean, I can lead a normal life."

I just nod.

Peggy goes back to dancing with her broom. She sings the ending of the song along with Elvis: "But lo-ove me-ee!"

33

My Explorer uniform hangs in the closet throughout the summer and fall, when I have to abandon *The New Hartford Frontier Register* and attend high school. Kathy sits with her friend Lynn Dery on the bus. I sit with Tim Krom. Girls sit on the left, boys on the right—not by edict but by choice. Occasionally, a boy will sneak in with a girl, or a girl will slide into a seat where a boy is sitting, but for the most part, we are bashfully segregated.

"Haven't seen you at Scouts this summer," Tim says. "Too busy being a newspaper editor?" His voice is tinged with something I think is sarcasm, but which he later tells me is grudging admiration.

"I guess so," I say. "But maybe I'll come back. I'm not doing the paper now."

Kathy is giggling with Lynn a few seats up and to our left. She's three steps away. She's continents away.

The next night, Dick Markwald shakes my hand as I walk into the Boy Scout meeting after an absence of four months. "Glad to have you back, Jack," he says. "Your Explorer uniform looks sharp."

As we salute the flag, a tall skinny kid nods at me and smiles. His khaki uniform hangs limp on him. The boy's face is pale and tired-looking.

"Baxter, that's a demerit for smiling during the Pledge," Dick says. "Troop, form the mill. Baxter, front and center."

I stand across from Tim in the mill lineup. The emaciated Bruce Baxter shuffles to the starting position. Dick whispers a few words to us about "going easy" on him. Bruce runs through the mill, and we all pretend to spank him. Hardly anyone makes contact, but Bruce stumbles and falls to his knees. He gets up laughing, shaking his head in mock embarrassment. I should rush to see if he's OK, but I don't. What if he tells me to beat it because I've been ignoring him all summer?

Dick takes Bruce aside and asks if he's hurt.

"I'm OK," I hear Bruce say. "Just a little weak. But I'm having another transfusion tomorrow, so I'll be stronger."

Four months later, in January 1961, Mrs. Baxter invites me to Bruce's fourteenth birthday party. I have no idea what to get for him.

"Why don't you give him the Explorer uniform for his birthday?" Mom suggests.

"But I need it!"

"Horse feathers," she says. "You haven't been to a meeting since September. He's old enough to wear it."

"Nah. I'll buy him a Superman comic or something."

"I'm sure the uniform would mean more," she says.

She's right, of course. John McGurk gets him a jar of marbles, Gil Coan gets him a whiffle ball and bat, and Tim Krom gets him a Superman comic book. He smiles at all of them, and then he opens my box. The uniform is pressed and neatly folded and packed in the original carton from Colt's, with the hat placed on top. Bruce's mouth drops open.

"You did this for me?" he says, overwhelmed.

"Wear it in good—wear it at tonight's meeting. I'll be there."

"I want to wear it forever," he says.

I go to the meeting, dressed in civvies, just to see Bruce dressed up in the uniform. His mother has let out the trouser cuffs just a bit, and it fits him perfectly. We sit together and thumb through his Scout manual. "We used to think something was funny about the pictures of these rope knots," Bruce says. "What was so funny?"

"I have no idea," I say.

"I've got something for you," he says. He hands me a sealed envelope. "But don't open it yet."

"OK. When should I open it?"

"Don't make me tell you," he says.

The rest of Bruce's time is taken up with hospital visits, tests, transfusions, missed school days. He sees another spring, survives the summer of 1961. When I begin my sophomore year at Regional, he starts his freshman year and rides the bus with me. Sometimes, he has to be helped on or off the bus. At the end of September, he tells me he is having another transfusion.

"You had one a week ago," I say.

On the morning of October 4, Gil Coan sits behind me on the bus and says, "Did you hear about Bruce?"

"Yeah, he's having a transfusion."

"He died yesterday," Gil says.

The bus driver pulls the folding doors closed and pulls away from our driveway. The cars that were stopped at the flashing red lights begin moving in the opposite direction. Out my window, the leaves are just turning yellow on the tree that Bruce learned was a maple more than five years ago. When the bus stops in Pine Meadow, Kathy and Lynn climb on and glance at me, glance away. Tim Krom heaves himself beside me in the seat and whispers, "You heard?" I just nod and gaze out the window, noticing the sample headstones in front of Bertolini's Monument Company. I feel Tim's hand on my shoulder. In the center of town, I gaze across the river at the firehouse where Bruce and Tim and I spent hours at Boy Scout meetings.

"Bruce," I mutter to no one.

Tim clears his throat. Gil says, "He was a good kid."

The lines of dark-suited men and veiled women snake around the parking lot at Shea's Funeral Home. There are uniformed Boy Scouts and Girl Scouts and other kids Bruce's age. Traffic is jammed at the intersection of Steele Road and Town Hill Road. It takes fifteen minutes for me to move close enough to see the body. When I finally see it, I gasp so quickly that I nearly choke on my own spittle.

Bruce Baxter is wearing my Explorer uniform.

He is buried the next day in a cemetery in Barkhamsted. The Scouts of Troop 39 form a sort of honor guard. I want to be with them, but I have no uniform, so I stand with Mom, Dad, Peggy, Ann, Tom, and Gerald.

Mr. Baxter squeezes Dad's shoulder when we approach them after the graveside service. Mrs. Baxter squeezes Mom's hand and attempts a joke: "Not a bad service for a Protestant minister, right Marion?"

Standing tall and straight and silent next to his parents is their remaining son, Greg, wiping tears from his eyes. His heart murmur is under control. He has outlived his older brother.

When I get home from the funeral, I take the envelope from my desk and slit it open with a Boy Scout jackknife, the kind with a black, plastic, faux leather handle. The blue-lined paper inside has been torn from a notebook.

"Look in the clubhouse," the paper says.

I walk across the old strawberry field and sneak into Bruce's tarpaper clubhouse. Impaled on a nail on the wall is a bulging manila envelope with my name on it. Inside is the Miraculous Medal I gave him, with this note:

Jack—I tried to make a miracle with this. It doesn't seem to be working. I'm not Catholic tho. Maybe it will work for you. Thanks for trying. Your friend Bruce.

34

Peggy has been fading from my life. When did we become separate people? When did she start ignoring me when she's with her friends, bickering with me at supper, fighting for the television program *she* wants to watch? Did it start with the flood? With her diabetes? With her boyfriends? With the skating rink? With Bruce?

What happened to the girl-mother who used to sing "Danny Boy" to me?

She wants to be a nurse, just like Mom, and after her 1962 high school graduation, she enrolls in Saint Francis School of Nursing in Hartford, the same school where Mom earned her RN in 1933. It is Mom who is closest to her now. Mom, who taught her how to treat her disease. Mom, who saved her life.

She's close to Dad, too. In October of 1962, the world almost blows up. Peggy calls Dad from her dormitory, terrified. "Yes, it is serious," Dad says into the phone. "No, I don't know what will happen. President Kennedy is on television right now, talking about blockading Cuba. I think it will be all right. Yes, I know you do. Yes, me too, dear."

Sometimes, she answers my letters. She scribbles them in longhand, during anatomy class, jokes about the parts of the body the nun is lecturing on today. Sometimes, she hands the letter to a classmate she has befriended, who writes something like, "Hi Jack! Are you cute?" The letters are surface thoughts of Peggy and her friends, nothing I can really touch.

Just once, there is a brief exchange that is really between Peggy and me. We make up stories about Froggy, our cat, give him a personality and a secret life, a secret room in the house. We call it the Frog Room. Only Froggy knows how to get to it, and it is filled with frogs, mushrooms, stalactites, glistening rock walls where spiders live, and a million mice that Froggy can catch and eat. When Froggy is nowhere to be found in the house, he must be in the Frog Room. It is a secret place known only to Froggy, Peggy, and me.

Our house in Puddletown gets to be too much for Dad to handle. The repairs after the flood were expensive. We're behind on the mortgage. In January 1963, we move back to Torrington, into the house where Mom grew up. "We're buying it from the estate of your mother's cousin," Dad tells us. "They're offering it to us at a very good price."

It's a house Peggy never really gets to live in, except on a few weekends and during Christmas and Easter breaks. It's a house that has torn me away from a support system of friends at Regional 7 High School and plopped me into a school three times the size, where I know nobody. I am seventeen years old, and I am trapped in a strange town, walled off by hills on all sides. Torrington, I learn, means City of the Ring of Hills.

Still, I move the imaginary Frog Room to Torrington, locate it somewhere under the upstairs linen closet.

On a Friday before Thanksgiving, I don't feel like going to school. I lie in bed with a slight cold, listening to the radio. A bulletin says that there were shots fired in Dallas, that President Kennedy's motorcade sped away, that more details would be forthcoming.

The nuns at Saint Mary's have taught me that miracles can happen. Jesus raised Lazarus from the dead. Jesus himself rose from the dead. As Kennedy's casket is paraded through Washington on black-and-white live television, I almost believe it is possible that the lid will open, the flag will flutter to the pavement, and a smiling Jack Kennedy will sit up, wave, then stand and smooth the wrinkles out of his suit.

In the spring of 1964, I ride my bicycle to New Hartford to visit Minnie and George Hough, who now live in a rented house in the Pine Meadow section. They are both now in their mid-seventies, and frail. "I quit drinking two years ago," George tells me, and Minnie nods, too weak to offer her nasal giggle. "I smoke Raleighs now, not Winstons. Look," he adds, opening a scrapbook displaying hundreds of Raleigh coupons. "You can get all kinds of prizes, you know?"

Two months later, George Hough dies of a stroke, almost nine years after he and Minnie crawled over from their floating house. I am one of the pallbearers. So is Mr. Kavanaugh, whose daughter Kathy never does become my girlfriend.

Peggy's boyfriend Ron usually drives her home from Hartford on Friday afternoons or late Friday nights. He parks his black VW bug in the driveway, keeps the engine running for twenty minutes, and finally the car door thuds and Peggy quietly lets herself into the house. Early Saturday mornings, Ron picks her up again, and they're gone all day. Sometimes, I get to drive her back to Hartford on Sunday nights. She looks out the passenger window. We don't say much.

I have an after-school and weekend job at Doyle's Pharmacy in Torrington, a store founded and run by Mom's cousin, Moses Doyle. On Sundays, I work a split shift, eight in the morning until noon and then six until ten at night. On a Sunday in August 1964, I nap between shifts, then jump out of bed at five-thirty p.m. I immediately wake up again on the floor of my bedroom, wondering how I got there. I dress hurriedly and go to work.

A week later, I again leap out of bed at five-thirty p.m. and get dressed, then run downstairs to use the bathroom. I wake up on the bathroom floor, looking up at the curvature of the porcelain bowl. Mom is banging on the door, asking what all the pounding is all about. "I think I passed out," I tell her.

Dr. Basile tells Dad, "Of *course* it's epilepsy. He had two grand mal seizures, didn't he? You saw the EEG results. I thought I had explained it all to you. He'll have to stay on Phenobarbital and Dilantin the rest of his life."

Peggy graduates from nursing school in 1965. She gets an apartment on Woodland Street in Hartford and works as a nurse at Saint Francis. I am out of high school and attending Northwestern Connecticut Community College, a new two-year school in Winsted.

Sometime around now, something goes wrong between Peggy and Ron. She has been seeing him fairly steadily since high school, where they were the most talked-about couple. They were the ones who were going to be happiest in their marriage—and a marriage was a foregone conclusion by most of their classmates. Ron is tall, square-jawed, blond, crew-cut, the only child of a wealthy industrialist who lived in an enormous white

Colonial mansion atop Town Hill in New Hartford. His yearbook picture is captioned, "Type of person who will go a long way if given the chance … considerate of others … friend of Peg's." Peggy's yearbook picture was captioned, "A cute little number … full of pep and energy … pal, Ronnie."

But even back in high school, it was not as it seemed. Ron was supposed to have appeared in a photo with Peggy in the Tallest and Shortest category. But instead, another tall senior boy appeared with Peggy in that photo. Was it because he was really taller than Ron? Or had Ron and Peggy had a temporary falling-out at picture-taking time?

Even more telling is Ron's message to Peggy under his picture in her yearbook: "Peg—best of luck in St. Francis and in your future. —Ron." He could have written "our future," or even "the future." But he conceded Peggy's whole future to Peggy—or Peg, as he and her other friends were beginning to call her.

But to most, it looked like a Cinderella story, and Peggy did not discourage the illusion. She never talked openly about their disagreements. She may have confided them to Mom, and Mom would have told Dad, but no one told anyone else. All we ever heard from Peggy was, "Ron bought me a necklace," or "Ron took me to a movie," or "Ron is so sweet."

It was impossible to ignore that Ron came from wealth. He dressed well, wore the expensive high school jacket with the big, gray-and-red embroidered letter, carried himself well, and greeted everyone with a wide, white smile and an honest handshake. His only rebellious practice was to drive a black VW bug, in the days when black VW bugs were still the People's Car. But this was not his father's VW bug—it was showroom-new, all paid for, and all Ron's.

Ron once let me tag along with him and Peggy in his little sailboat. He taught me about tacking. "It is actually possible to sail into the wind," he said. "You can't do it directly, of course. You have to zigzag. But look, we're doing it. The wind is blowing in our faces, but I can use this wind to reach the shore in front of us."

Peggy just smiled, blissfully unaware that she would be zigzagging against the wind for five years, waiting for Ron to propose, waiting to break out of poverty and marry a decent man with a decent fortune.

Sometime in 1966, it all falls apart. Peggy is finished with schooling, and she is working at Saint Francis as a nurse. I am still at NCCC, the community college in Winsted, living a life apart from the rest of the family. On my occasional weekend visits with Peggy, she seems quieter, and she stays in the house. Ron doesn't call or drop by.

"What happened to Ron?" I ask her one day.

"We broke up," is all she says.

Decades later, Dad will tell me that he helped bring the courtship to an end. "I called Ron's father one day," Dad will tell me. "I told him I didn't think a marriage would be a good idea. I could not pay for the kind of wedding their family would want to have, and I thought there would be only resentment between the families because of the financial differences. Marrying outside your station doesn't work."

In late October, few months after the breakup, Dad drives Peggy back to her apartment after a weekend visit to Torrington. I sit in the backseat with Peggy, who now is going with a man named Richard. "I have a secret," she says to me, smiling.

"What?"

She shows me a ring on her finger.

"You're engaged?"

She shakes her head and smiles again. She pats her stomach.

"No. Really?"

She nods. "I just got married!"

The most surprising thing is that Peggy seems happy—quietly, serenely happy. "It's wonderful," she says. "Isn't it wonderful?"

There is nothing to say. Something terrifying and irrevocable has happened, and she welcomes it. I hear the echo of her words from six years ago: *"I'm going to be OK, you know ... I can lead a normal life."*

A few months later, our cat Froggy dies. The secrets of the Frog Room are lost forever. We never speak of it again.

35

Mom and I are both crying in the dining room in the Torrington homestead.

"We haven't really lost her," Mom says. "I think Dick is a fine man and a hard worker. He can give her a good life."

"But they just ran off and got married, in secret," I say. "One minute she's here, then she's off getting—getting pregnant and—eloping!"

Mom sits at the Hitchcock table and studies the stenciling. The dinette set—table, eight chairs and a hutch—is an extravagance she allowed herself a couple years ago, after her uncle died and left her a small inheritance. Dad's spotty income from selling hearing aids rarely allows her to acquire such things. Mom knows how to make the most of a small advantage.

"She may have married Dick on the rebound," Mom says. "Dick can't give her what Ron could have given her, but he's still a hard worker."

Mom doesn't even believe her own words, I am thinking. What happened to the outrage she showed a few years ago when one of Peggy's girlfriends "went to visit relatives out of state" for several months and then "had the nerve to come back and bring that illegitimate child to Sunday Mass!" What kind of doublethink goes through a mother's mind when her own daughter does the same thing?

"I don't even know him," I say. "It feels like she's gone away somewhere."

"I know. But he's part of the family now. We must pray for them and the baby, that they will be happy." She tries to hide her tears but can't. She brushes a crumb from the Hitchcock table.

Sean is born in January 1967. Peggy chooses my brother Gerald as godfather, and I feel just a bit slighted. "I was going to ask you to be godfather," she says to me one day, "but he looked just like Gerald's baby picture."

It is coming up on Spring Weekend at NCCC. I have a date with Laura Hanson, and I don't quite know how I managed it. Laura is sleek and slim; has long blond hair; and has dated mostly tall, virile, muscular men. But she just broke up with a guy she'd been seeing for months, the guy everyone thought she'd marry, and as she passes me in the hall one day, she smiles at me.

"Dan says you're staying with him and Don, here in Winsted," she says, tilting her head and smiling.

"What? Oh, right," I say. "It's better for everyone. I can walk to school, and I help with their rent."

"I'd like to see the house," she says.

My friends Dan and Don rent a house on Stanton Avenue for twenty-four dollars a week. I pay them eight dollars a week and get the spare bedroom at the top of the stairs.

"Laura Hanson wants to visit me here tonight," I tell Dan.

Dan's eyes widen. "Laura Hanson? Isn't she going with What's-His-Name? Bob?"

"They just broke up. And we're going to Spring Weekend dance on Saturday, too."

"Hoo, this I gotta see," Dan says. "She's definitely—pardon me for saying it—a notch above you."

"You're a real pal, Dan."

"Hey, I could be wrong. If you get to carve a notch in the bedpost tonight, I'll take it all back."

That night, Laura wears a thigh-high, tight red skirt and a white blouse with the top two buttons unbuttoned. We sit on the living room couch drinking Schlitz from cans. Dan and Don eyeball us from time to time, then drift out of the room and out of sight.

I put Chubby Checker on the turntable, and Laura and I twist. Then I look for slower music and find only early Beatles and Rolling Stones. Finally, I find a radio station that plays the slower Elvis tunes. I push the coffee table to the edge of the room and put my arm around Laura's tiny waist. She kicks off her shoes and bends her knees slightly. This has two marvelous effects. It makes her shorter, so she is no longer two inches taller than me, and it causes her knees to brush against my legs.

Laura reaches for the light switch and turns it off. The room is dark except for the glow of the radio dial and a streetlamp filtering through a torn shade. We are cheek to cheek to "Love Me Tender," and I'm grateful now for Peggy's dance lessons. But now I do something I would never have done with Peggy. I drop Laura's hand and put both arms around her. Our feet stop dancing and we keep swaying. Her cheek slides against mine until our lips touch. She holds my head with both hands, and her tongue slides into my mouth. The universe is quaking, and time is standing still.

"I can stay as long as you want," she whispers.

"Oh good," I whisper, and I kiss her with my tongue.

We keep dancing for five minutes, fifteen minutes, and Laura lets out a sigh.

"What do you want to do?" she says.

"Just be with you," I tell her.

"Do you want me to stay?"

"Of course."

Dan enters and clears his throat. "Um, excuse me, Jack and Laura, but Don and I are going out to the V.D. Do you mind?"

He's talking about the Valley Diner, a rounded, chrome-plated, all-night ham-and-egg place on the road between Winsted and New Hartford. Its venereal reputation is unearned and unfair, but we figure it serves the place right for not thinking the name through.

"OK with me," Laura smiles.

"Sure," I say. "You want company?"

Don comes in and gives a little head shake. Dan looks puzzled. "Company?"

I look at Laura. "Want to get a coffee at the V.D.?"

Elvis is singing the final lines of a song: "Tell me dear, are you lonesome tonight?" There is a second of dead air before the mood is broken by a commercial for Chock full o'Nuts Coffee.

Truth is, I am running out of ideas to entertain Laura. Never mind what I really want to do. What about afterwards? Will she say she didn't really want to do it? Is this a girl I would want to marry, if I had to marry someone? Is she even Catholic? A Democrat? And never mind all that, what if she gets pregnant? I'm still in college, no job. It's bad enough that Peggy had to get married, but at least she and Dick are both out of school and both working.

The radio sings, "Better coffee a millionaire's money—" and Laura reaches over and flicks it off, then flicks on the light. The silence echoes, the light blinds me. "Sure," she says. "Great. Fine. Let's get a coffee."

That Saturday, on our date at Spring Weekend, Laura leaves me alone on the dance floor and takes over the concession table, cheerfully serving strawberry punch in Dixie cups to thirsty dancers. "It's just for a few minutes," she tells me. But she stays there for an hour, and I finally look around for someone to dance with. I latch onto Emily Larkin, a cute, short brunette, Laura's best friend, but we dance only once before she finds another guy. Eventually, a tall, virile, muscular man asks Laura to dance, and she abandons the concession table, kicks off her shoes, bends her knees, and dances while Brenda Lee sings "Break It to Me Gently."

36

In the Summer of Love, the Vietnam War rages on. The Beatles have just released a new album. Five American League baseball teams are within inches of each other for the lead in the pennant race. I am on summer break from NCCC, and my friend Gil Hebberd has just received his associate's degree from there. The two of us are playing chess by mail. I have just taken his black king pawn with my white knight, and if he recaptures my knight with his, I will fork his knight and bishop with my queen's pawn.

Thursday, July 24, 1967: I call Gil and suggest a swim at Highland Lake in Winsted. "Maybe Emily and Laura would want to come with us," I add. Laura and I have reached a let's-just-be-friends agreement, no hard feelings.

He arrives in his old station wagon in late morning. I toss my towel in the back and slide across the vinyl passenger seat.

"I mailed my chess move to you a couple days ago," I say.

"I got it," he says, nodding, smiling mysteriously. "Interesting move. I sent you the reply this morning."

Sitting behind the wheel, Gil appears tall and lanky, like a young Jimmy Stewart. He even smokes a pipe occasionally, though not today. He moves and speaks slowly, but his mind is quick. He is one of my most formidable chess opponents, though in the present correspondence game, I hold a slight edge.

The girls are waiting for us at Emily's house in Winsted. They invite us in to show off Emily's new *Sgt. Pepper's Lonely Hearts Club Band* album. "Check this out!" Emily says, putting the record on the turntable.

"What do you see when you turn out the light? I can't tell you, but I know it's mine," sing the Beatles.

At Highland Lake, I am the first to test the waters. I dive in at Holland Beach and nearly lose my trunks, which are a bit too big for me. "It's kind of shallow here," I say, secretly tightening my drawstring. "Let's swim the cove."

We pay no attention to the No Swimming sign. Shadows of overhanging trees give Woodland Cove an ominous appearance. We take turns swinging out over the water on a rope suspended from a tree limb. Emily and Laura then swim to the other side, some sixty yards away.

"Ready, Gil?" I say. "I'll race you."

"Oh, I don't know," he says. "I think I'll walk around and meet you over there."

"Oh, come on!" I tease. "It's not far."

I dive in, swim a third of the way under water, enjoying the darkness, the stillness. I surface to see Gil paddling strongly behind me.

"See, it's not bad!" I say. "Hey, if you drown, I'll forfeit the chess game to you."

When I reach the other side, the girls are happily cannonballing off a pier. As I walk up the stone steps, I notice something in the water beside me.

"Hey, look at the turtle!"

The girls scamper over and poke at the six-inch long amphibian for a couple minutes, wondering if it is a snapper. I say I don't think so.

"Where's Gil?" Laura asks.

"Oh, he's right behind me, he's coming."

"I don't see him."

"Where is he?" Emily's voice is edged with alarm.

Now we see the top of a young man's head bobbing in the water and his right arm reaching up, reaching up.

"It's Gil!" Laura says.

"That's not him!" Emily says. "Where's Gil?"

Not him? I think. *Is it OK if it's somebody else?*

"What's he doing?" Laura screams.

A black boy about eight years old is leaning against a boat house, sipping a Coke through a bent straw. "He's drowning," the boy says. He takes a sip.

Gil's head and hand disappear, and we see bubbles. We all stand there, disbelieving.

Of course, we don't just stand there. Emily and Laura are screaming, the black boy is slurping his Coke, and my heart is pounding. I am still worried that I might lose my swimming trunks if I dive in to save Gil. I don't want to be a naked hero.

I don't know how long it takes for me to try it anyway, but when I reach the spot where he went under, about twenty feet off shore, I find nothing. The water is at least ten feet deep, and murky.

Emily and Laura find a tattered wooden raft near the boathouse, and they paddle around on it for several minutes, looking under the surface.

It feels like ten minutes since Gil has disappeared, but maybe it's only two or three. I try another dive—and there he is! He is lying face down on the bottom with his arms outstretched. It is an effort to get down that deep, but I finally grab his wrist. I pull him up, and he comes up easily. This is a relief. I have Gil, and he is coming up easily.

I surface, my lungs bursting. "I've got him!" I call.

"Where?" Laura asks, paddling the raft toward me. There is a buzzing in my ears, and I can barely hear her.

"I've got his wrist! Keep the raft away, you'll bump him!"

"Get his head above water!" she yells.

I try to pull him up, but his weight is displacing me, and I am sinking.

"Get his head above water!" Laura yells again.

The buzzing in my ears is nearly as loud as her shrieking. I pull again, go under again, and decide to just try dragging him to shore under water.

"Get his head above water!" Laura yells one more time.

I try one more time. His wrist slips away from me.

"I lost him!" I say.

"What?!" Emily shouts.

"He's gone!"

The buzzing stops, and the stillness is even louder.

The girls jump off the raft and we all dive for him, but we can't find him. By now, I am exhausted from fright and exertion, and I have to head for shore to save my own life. Emily and Laura continue looking. The boy with the Coke is saying we should call the cops.

The police find Gil about thirty yards from where he slipped from my grasp, carried by a tricky current. As they put his putty-colored form on a stretcher, someone from the gathering crowd says, "Oh, he's gone."

A cop shouts into his radio. "Possible ten-thirty-two! I need a nine-oh-one-B to Woodland Cove, nine-oh-one-B! Young male victim." The radio crackles back, "Roger, fourteen, out."

The cops put a resuscitator over Gil's mouth, and the gurgling sound makes Laura vomit. An ambulance screams into the driveway and paramedics whisk Gil away in less than ten seconds.

Emily has Gil's car keys and drives Laura and me to Winsted Memorial Hospital. Laura says, "That damn black bastard kid, he just stood there!" *But he's eight years old*, I am thinking. *What's our excuse?*

At the hospital, no one will tell us anything. We leave Gil's car there, and the cops drive us to the station to get our statements.

The black telephone on the cop's desk rings like a fire alarm. "Sergeant Whyte here." A quick glance at the three young people in swimsuits, then a curt, "Understood. Do a ten-fifty-five-D." He drops the heavy receiver to its cradle.

"What's a ten-fifty-five-D?" Emily says.

The cop takes a breath. "It means call the coroner. I'm sorry."

The police offer to drive us home. They drive us to Torrington first to drop me off. Laura spends the trip looking out the window and crying silently. Emily takes my hand. As I get out at my house, she kisses me, a quick and desperate kiss.

The house is empty. The silence and aloneness make the day's events seem like a dream. I turn on the radio, just for distraction. The Beatles are singing, *"How do you feel by the end of the day? Are you sad because you're on your own?"*

The next day, an envelope arrives in the mail. It's from Gil. As commander of the black pieces, his chess move is just three letters: "NxN"—knight takes knight. I take my pen and carefully print beneath his move, "White resigns."

37

For several weeks after Gil's death, Emily, Laura and I hang around together, a sort of guilty survivors' support group. I worry that we will be arrested, charged with some kind of crime: negligent homicide, manslaughter, failure to report an emergency. We frighten each other with scenarios of courtroom shackles, orange jump suits, a frowning judge, hissing jurors, and an incompetent public defender recommending we plead guilty to some lesser charge that will get us out within five years. We are terrified, even when our parents and friends tell us we did all we could, nothing could have happened differently, we are not to blame.

We know better. I should never have insisted Gil swim the cove after he told me he didn't want to. Or, I should have swum beside him, like Red Cross instruction taught me. We should have kept an eye on him, and on each other. There was a pay phone right near the cove, and we didn't call until it was too late. The list of "know betters" goes on and on.

The Summer of Love ends, and Laura and Emily drift out of my life. My British lit teacher is the yearbook advisor, and he dedicates the book to Gil Hebberd. I occupy myself less with college that fall than with chessplaying and following the Red Sox, who almost—but only almost—win the World Series that October.

Now it is the spring of 1968, and an ad in the *Courant* classifieds catches my eye: "Part time reporter wanted. Contact J. O'Brien."

"Type this," Joe O'Brien says, handing me a press release about Winsted's annual Laurel Festival, a small-town beauty pageant. He is the same Joe O'Brien who interviewed me eight years ago about my family newspaper.

I bang out the press release pretty quickly.

"Okay, but it's got to be all caps. And if you have to make a lowercase letter, like the C in McDonald, you just leave a space after the C. Got it? The teletype machine only does uppercase. They retype the stories at the state desk in Hartford. I thought you said you studied journalism in college." Joe's voice has the staccato rhythm of a typewriter. With every quick breath, you can almost hear the ding of a carriage return, then the bang-bang-bang of the next relentless sentence.

"I did," I say. "They taught us the five W's. Nothing about teletype."

He takes a quick drag on his Winston. "They don't teach you what you need. I had a kid in here last year, covering the Laurel Festival. He started to write some crap about 'A bevy of beautiful girls' and so on. Don't do that. You may think they're beautiful, but it's not for you to decide. Got it?"

"I think so."

"Okay, let's get some coffee and I'll get you started. How do you like your coffee?"

I think for a second. "Light," I say. "With half a sugar."

He squints at me and looks away. The woman sending a story on the teletype stops typing. "That's just how Joe takes his coffee," she says.

For the next three months, Joe and I work side by side, sometimes enjoying each other's company, sometimes getting on each other's nerves. He sends me out to cover minor meetings, like the organization of a teen center at Rowley Park. I write about blueberry festivals and recreation department schedule changes. I call the police station several times a day to get the latest arrests from their blotter. I also take the town correspondents' stories over the phone, retyping as they dictate. Then I do some minor editing before handing the stories to the teletypist to retype, so the state desk can mark them up or type them yet again and send them to compositing for a final typeset. One of the correspondents is my former high school English teacher. Now I am correcting her papers, and that makes me smile.

Joe keeps the important stories for himself. When the local school superintendent is fired during an executive session, he delves into it, unearthing all the juicy tidbits. Then, at a later school board meeting we cover together, a board member criticizes Joe for referring to executive sessions as "secret meetings." "They're not secret," the man insists. "I wish you would look up the meaning of secret."

Joe looks it up. A dozen dictionaries define the word as "withheld from public view" or "hidden." With a gleam in his eye, he files a story that appears the next morning under the headline, "Reporter Asked Not to Call Secret Meetings 'Secret.'"

On a slow Saturday afternoon, Joe and I scramble around trying to figure out how to fill fifty inches of newsprint when nothing is happening. Suddenly, he is on the phone, talking to elected officials, registrars of voters and city hall workers. "Who's going to run for office this year?" is the theme of his roundup story. He files about twenty-five inches, a story conjured up like a magician's dove, researched entirely in one afternoon from his squeaky swivel chair and a big black telephone.

I am in awe of Joe O'Brien. He can make a story out of thin air and just as easily let the wind out of an overblown press release. He manages to expose wrongdoing by town officials and stay on good terms with most of his contacts, balancing on that tightrope all good reporters must walk. By the time I leave his employ in August 1968, to attend college in Wisconsin, I have learned more about journalism than in four years of high school and three years of college.

One day during that summer of 1968, while Joe and I are balling up bad story drafts and missing the waste baskets, I ask if he remembers interviewing me about my own little newspaper eight years ago. "Of course," he says. "That's why—" and he stops talking and starts typing again.

Watch it, Joe, I think. *You almost paid me a compliment.*

On my last day, I treat him to a coffee. Light, with half a sugar. And I wonder why I ordered mine that way my first day on the job three months ago. That's not how I take my coffee. I like it dark, no sugar.

Another year drifts by. Pheromones from half a continent away summon me back early to Superior, Wisconsin, at the end of August 1969. The all-consuming memory of a late-night waltz with a woman I'll call Charlene has not left me alone all summer. The night before I was to leave the Superior campus of Wisconsin State University to return home for summer break, I visited Charlene's third-floor walkup on Belknap, helped put her two young boys to bed, and turned on the record player. We swayed to Dean Martin's rendition of "The Green, Green Grass of Home." Our bodies were crying for each other, and we danced for hours.

Two months later, back home in Connecticut, the unfulfilled promise of that dance still aches. I tell Dad I need to get back early to put a deposit on my off-campus apartment. He massages his chin, like Doc on "Gunsmoke," and walks away.

The next morning, Friday, August 29, he appears in my bedroom as I am dressing. "I took a few days off from the office," he says. "Can you be packed by tomorrow morning? We'll start driving to Wisconsin after breakfast."

Most of my belongings cram into a small footlocker which slides into the trunk of Dad's snappy, red 1966 Volvo 1800S. On the New York State Thruway, Dad turns the driving over to me. All I am thinking of is getting to Superior *now*, so I can see Charlene *now*. In a sixty-five-mile-an-hour zone, the New York State Police radar clocks me at eighty-two. A sunburned cop smiles as he hands me a ticket, and Dad takes back the wheel.

The first day gets us all the way across New York State, about three hundred seventy-five miles from Torrington, and we stay the night in a forgettable motel in Buffalo. I care nothing for the trip—only the destination—and I secretly rejoice to see the edge of Lake Erie from the motel window, knowing I am only three Great Lakes away from Charlene.

The next morning, August 31, is a Sunday, which probably explains why we drive only about three hundred miles this day. No doubt we get up late, eat breakfast in a nearby Howard Johnson's or some such place, and find a Catholic church to attend Mass. Then we hop back on Interstate 90, now called the Ohio Turnpike, and drive along the southern edge of Lake Erie. On my turn at the wheel, I let the Volvo's right-hand wheels veer off onto a gravel shoulder at a high speed, and the car lurches back to the left and crosses a lane of traffic before I can regain control, barely missing an oncoming car. I pull over, and we sit staring straight ahead, hearts racing. We open our doors at the same time, get out, and meet in front of the car. "Nice recovery," he manages to say.

"Your driving lessons didn't mention gravel shoulders. But I did effect a cessation, didn't I?"

We smile. I sit in the passenger's seat. Dad takes the wheel.

The only memorable detail about the motel in Toledo is the long, kidney-shaped indoor swimming pool. Dad and I change into our swimming trunks and claim a couple of chairs at one narrow end of the kidney. Dad dives in and swims the length and back.

"Are you coming in?" he asks.

"I don't know," I say. "It's been a long time."

Dad's face changes, and he pulls himself out, letting the pool drain from his hairy, pink skin. "Is that what's bothering you on this trip?" he asks. "After more than two years? You know it wasn't your fault."

I do not want to talk about what is really bothering me, because Dad is dead set against my relationship with Charlene.

"I guess so," I say. "I just don't seem to have any desire to swim anymore."

Now Dad seems relieved to be able to enter into his role as father. He pauses, perhaps relishing the moment. "I think I understand," he finally says. "There were times when I was a boy when I nearly capsized my dory in Salem Harbor while no one was around. I could have disappeared. No one would have found me."

"It's not that. I'm not afraid of drowning."

"What, then?"

"I had him."

"You did all you could."

"That's what everybody says. But all I can think of is feeling his wrist in my fist, and then not feeling it. It plays like a scene from a movie, over and over. I can't even imagine a different ending anymore. I can't imagine getting him to shore and giving him mouth-to-mouth or anything. All I can imagine is what really happened. I had him, and then I didn't."

Dad doesn't say anything for a long time. "Remember the night at the funeral home?" he finally says. "I went to talk to Gil's father, to pay my condolences. All he could say was, 'Yes, it's a great loss. My wife just died a few months ago, Gil's mother, and now this. A great, great loss.' He asked you what happened, and you told him, and he looked down at you with a tear in his eye. This tear was for you, Jack. He had shed a thousand tears for his wife, a thousand more for his son, and he still had one left for you. Do you understand?"

I am wishing I had clothes on so I can reach for a handkerchief to blow my nose. I blink back the mist so I can see my father's face. "Dad," I say, "I saw him ten feet under me. He was probably still alive. I dove down and got him. I had him in my hand. And then I lost him."

"What do you wish for more than anything?" Dad says.

I know he is thinking I wish Gil were still alive, and I do; but what do I wish for more than anything? The pheromones are stronger than ever, now only two Great Lakes away. I don't dare discuss this with my Jesuit-taught father from the Puritan state of Massachusetts. He will read my silence according to his own lights, I am thinking; but please don't let him lecture me about God's will.

"Whatever that is," he continues, "time will help it to pass. The unattainable the mind lets go eventually. You're only twenty-three, so this doesn't make sense yet, but it's really true. Meanwhile, you have to bring yourself back to life."

I am sitting on the edge of the pool, dangling my feet in the cool water. Is he talking about Gil, or does he know what I'm really wishing for?

Without a word, Dad dives in and treads water, just looking at me from fifteen feet away. Now, exactly eight hundred days after Gil's drowning, I jump in, swim underwater in the darkness, the stillness. I surface alongside my father and resist the urge to look behind me, knowing no one is paddling frantically to reach me. Dad and I swim to the other end of the pool, and we reach it at the same moment.

38

At a filling station near Elkhart, Indiana, a newspaper kiosk displays a story commemorating the thirtieth anniversary of Hitler's invasion of Poland. "I remember that dark day," Dad says as the man behind the Texaco star squeegees our windshield. "I wasn't much older than you are now. Twenty-six, I believe. I was four years out of college and floundering, trying to find something better to do than sell life insurance door to door. It was still the Depression, remember. When war came to Europe, a lot of people worried it would come here too. At the very least, it got some of us thinking about things outside of ourselves."

Again with the lessons, I am thinking. *Everything's a Goddamn lesson*. I grunt and pretend to study a Texaco road map of northern Indiana.

We cover a lot of miles this day. In Chicago, we finally veer northward onto I-94 and invade Wisconsin just after lunch. Lake Michigan is on our right all the way to Milwaukee. Another two hours later, due west of Milwaukee, we see the shining capitol dome in Madison. We keep driving. At a railroad crossing, we sit watching a mile-long Soo Line freight train rumble past. "Think of it," Dad says, apropos of nothing at all. "How easy it would be to disappear."

The caboose rattles past, the gate swings up, the bells and lights are still. A horn behind us prompts Dad to resume driving.

139

As night falls, we collapse into warm beds in a Holiday Inn in Eau Claire. We have logged more than six hundred fifty miles this day, and we are only a hundred fifty miles from the campus in Superior.

Tuesday, September 2, 1969: Determined to reach Superior by ten in the morning, we are dressed by six-thirty, finished with a quick breakfast of French toast in the Holiday Inn's restaurant by seven-fifteen, and on Route 53 by seven-forty-five. "Welcome to Chippewa Falls," the first sign proclaims at eight o'clock. "Entering New Auburn, Wisconsin," another sign says at eight-thirty. We glide through Rice Lake, Sarona, Trigo, Minong, Gordon, and Solon Springs—towns that are no more than black-and-white signboard proclamations. In Wentworth, at nine-fifty-five, a proclamation reads: "Superior 16 miles."

Along Tower Avenue in Superior, every storefront takes full advantage of the city's unique name. There is a Superior Records, selling, one would assume, better vinyl discs than anyone else. There is a Superior Typewriter & Repair, whose merchandise and service must be second to none. Even the *Superior Evening Telegram* implies that it is a better newspaper than any other *Evening Telegram* in the nation.

"Dad, remember the name of the place in Torrington where I worked this summer? Superior Building Maintenance and Supply Company. It's the only business in Torrington that uses the word 'Superior' in its name. Here, they all do."

"Well, we're right on the western tip of Lake Superior," Dad says. "It's not amazing. What's amazing is why you chose to work at Superior Building Maintenance and Supply Company. You could have worked as a reporter for *The Hartford Courant* again, like last summer. You seem to be obsessed with this city."

"*The Courant* wasn't hiring," I remind him.

He ignores this. "Well, let's get you settled in. Where's your apartment?"

We climb the steps of a duplex at 1612 North 16th Street, where the landlord tells us the apartment is still occupied and won't be ready for two weeks.

"What do you mean it's not ready?" Dad demands. "We just drove halfway across the continent to move my son into this apartment."

The landlord shrugs.

"Never mind," I tell Dad as we walk back to the car. "I think Ed Boyle will put me up for a couple nights. He's a friend of mine, lives down by the freight yard."

"Bad section of town? I hope not. He's not a radical hippie type, is he?"

"No, no, it's a nice house."

Bewhiskered Ed Boyle, a copy of *New Left News* tucked under his arm, is a bit surprised to see me, but he welcomes me into a spare bedroom. Then Dad and I run some errands, setting up a bank account for me and drawing from it a certified check to send by registered mail to the New York State judicial system for my speeding ticket. Then we explore the campus before Dad has to turn around and head home.

Charlene is so close I can taste her, and I don't know how to contain myself. I am constantly looking out the car window as we drive up Belknap, past her apartment above People's Drug—presumably another pharmacy was already named Superior Drug—and onto the WSU-Superior campus on Catlin Avenue. No sign of Charlene. We park near the Rothwell Student Center and explore the tree-lined green in front of Old Main, the original classroom building dating back to 1893. We roam through McCaskin Hall, where most of the classrooms and labs are, and back out to the walkways. I see a female student wearing a green jacket just like one Charlene owns, but it is not Charlene.

I treat Dad to a coffee in the Rothwell Student Center. Coffees are served in flimsy white cones supported by brown plastic holders. You're supposed to throw away the cone and return the holder when you're done. We sit by ourselves at a long table. Dad is looking around, impressed with my campus, and I am looking around, pretending not to be searching every face for the one I came to see.

"You can't stop thinking of her, can you?" he says.

I decide not to be surprised. "I know you don't approve," I say. "But you know, we're just friends. We're not—we never—well, we're not really serious."

"She's divorced. She's older than you. She has two kids," Dad says. "And she's Protestant." *Ooh, the clincher.*

A female student recognizes me and flashes a smile. I wave and say, "Hi, Colleen!" I try not to be embarrassed to be sitting with my fifty-six-year-old father, but I feel divided between two worlds. "That's Colleen Sweeney," I tell Dad. Then, perversely, I add: "Nice, single, virginal, Irish Catholic girl."

He studies his coffee. Johnny Cash is singing from the jukebox: *"... threw down my gun, / called him my pa, and he called me his son..."*

We finish the coffees without another word. We walk back to the red Volvo without making eye contact. "Well, son," Dad says, not wanting to drive away from me just yet.

"Dad," I interrupt, "thanks for driving out here with me. I just—can I ask one quick favor? I just want to show off this car for Charlene. Just for a minute. Can you—could you maybe stay here for about ten minutes while I—?"

"No, Jack. This is not a good thing. If you are really not serious about her, you should stop seeing her. Let go of things that are not yours. Now I'd better get going before I start to cry."

I suddenly realize the extent of my obsession. I would have left my father alone, without transportation, in a strange city, just to see a girl who barely wrote me all summer.

Embarrassed, I give my father a quick kiss on the cheek, and he closes the car door behind him. "I'll be fine," I tell him. "Ed will let me stay until the apartment is ready."

"Goodbye, my son."

"I love you, Dad. Drive safely—not like me."

He waves once and eases the car into first gear. As he turns left onto Belknap, I realize I am still holding a brown plastic coffee cup holder.

39

As the sleek red Volvo disappears around the corner, I glance at my watch. It's four p.m. already. I have been in Superior for six hours, showing Dad around, waiting to see Charlene. I start walking toward her apartment above People's Drug, thinking of how we met.

Going away to college was scary a year earlier, but exciting. Gil's death plunged me into a depression that lasted months. I played chess all the time instead of attending classes at NCCC. I read virtually no books, did virtually no schoolwork. Finally, on the advice of the assistant dean, I dropped out, "until you can see the value of a college education."

A friend told me about Wisconsin State. Tuition was cheap, and applying was free. Plus, they had a great English department. To my surprise, they accepted me on probation.

But Ross Hall Dormitory proved unsuitable for studying. False fire alarms punctured the night during the fall 1968 semester. You didn't dare answer a knock on your door, for fear a bucket of water would flood your room. You didn't dare sleep in an unlocked room, for fear your wrist would be placed in warm water, making you wet your bed. Some of the least offensive entertainment was gathering around to watch a fat kid light his farts on fire.

The second semester, I escaped to Sundquist Hall, closer to campus. A kid with a beard showed me an essay titled "The Student as Nigger." It was the beginning of my induction—or indoctrination—into the New Left. By being made to feel oppressed, I could sympathize with those who were more oppressed.

It was the perfect setup for succumbing to someone like Charlene.

She had a full blond wig that I thought for the longest time was her real hair. She approached me from across a crowded student union one day in May 1969. "Someone said you type papers for twenty-five cents a page," she said, her deep brown eyes pleading with me.

"Yes, sometimes," I said.

"I'm on welfare. I can't pay you. But if you bring your typewriter to my apartment, I can make supper for you."

The typewriter stayed at her apartment for four months. Turned out, I had to write her papers, not just type them, since her spelling was atrocious and her grammar even worse. On the first visit, when it came time to feed me as promised, she "discovered" all she had were two hot dogs, and her two young boys hadn't eaten supper yet. So I bought us a snack at the Patio Café next door to People's. And I bought a small jar of Maxim instant coffee.

Some nights, we would share a six-pack of Blatt's Beer. Most of the time, she talked, piercing me with her eyes and her stories about an abusive ex-husband; the difficulties of raising two kids alone; her boyfriend, Dusty, in the Navy, who kept promising to leave his wife; and the hopeless struggle against the Douglas County Welfare Department.

There were other men who did favors for Charlene. "But they all want something in return," she would say. "Jim Spencer wants me to clean his apartment for him. Do all men expect something in return?"

Trying to understand a mind like Charlene's became a challenge. Her philosophy seemed to be: *Why should a gift giver expect payment? Besides, I made coffee, didn't I?*

Coffee the gift giver bought for her.

Many men helped her with schoolwork, lent her money, or just bought her gifts to try to get laid, but I was the only one who tried to listen. I must have thought she had something to say that I could do something about. The small gifts I bought for her—coffee, Hamburger Helper, a carton of Kool cigarettes for Mother's Day—were gifts of pity. Payment was watching her eyes light up when she received them. No other payment was expected. My Catholic upbringing made me fear asking for the kind of payment most men would ask for, and I didn't dare hint about it.

For this, I earned an unusual compliment: "You really are among the top twenty percent of men who give more than they ask. Do you know how rare that is?"

Did she know how dangerous that compliment was? Probably she did. It kept the gifts coming for many more months.

Now People's Drug Store is right in front of me. It is four-fifteen p.m. on my first day back in Superior. I should buy her a box of candy or something before going upstairs to her apartment.

"Hi, Jack!" a skinny young man shouts, and everyone in the drugstore turns to look at us. It is Melvin Fairweather, black eyes magnified by thick glasses, face contorted into his perpetual grin. He is wearing a knee-length, psychedelic pullover shirt swirling with colors.

"Hi, Melvin," I say, then look away, knowing I must escape.

"So how ya been? Just got back? Whatcha up to?"

"Um, not much. Just going to see Charlene."

"Oh, Charlene! Yeah! Me too! Come on, we'll both go."

"Uh, that's OK. I haven't seen her all summer, you know. You understand."

"But I was on my way up there myself just now," he says. He continues talking while I follow him out the door and toward the back of the building. As we are climbing the wooden stairs toward the apartment, he is saying, "I've been hanging around with her a lot this summer. Hey, guess what! I'm stoned on acid. I scored it at Woodstock this summer. Were you there? It's right near you on the East Coast. Did you go? I didn't see you. Of course there were thousands of people. You should have gone. I told Charlene about it. She didn't go either, but that's understandable. I mean, how could she go? She can't afford to walk across the street, ha ha ha! I got this shirt there, too. What do you think?"

We have arrived at Charlene's door. This is not how I imagined our reunion, as a tag-along to a tripping, crazy homosexual kid in a muumuu by Jackson Pollock.

Melvin knocks at the door. "Charlene? Hey, are you home?"

"Melvin," I protest, "you didn't have to come with—"

"No problem, Jack. Hey, maybe she's on the roof."

We climb up to the roof, but no one is there. Charlene's pink panties are hanging on a clothesline, and I try to look away.

"Come with me to the student union, maybe she's there," he says as we reach the sidewalk.

"Melvin, I've got to go."

"Where?"

"I'm staying with Ed Boyle."

"Oh, me too! I'll walk with you."

This can't be happening, I'm thinking. *Why is this weird kid hanging around me? He doesn't like Charlene, and he doesn't live with Ed Boyle. I don't want to share my footsteps with him any longer.*

"Melvin, I don't need—"

"Are you hungry? Did you eat yet? Let's try the Patio. Or, hey, let's go to the student union. The food's bad, but there's people there. You got a smoke, Jack? I'm all out. Hey, let's get a drink. If you want, I can score some pot. I think I even have some stashed somewhere. I can't remember where. How much money you got? We'll buy some more. Maybe get some Ripple or Boones Farm with it. You're not in a hurry, right?"

"Hey Melvin, I don't have any money, OK?"

He blinks. "You don't? It's your first day back, right?"

"Uh, right."

"How did you get here with no money? You need to pay tuition, don't you?"

"It's prepaid," I lie. "It's taken care of. So I don't have any money for beer or wine or pot or food. Sorry, Melvin."

"Oh, so you think that's it? So that's what? That's not it, you know. I just wanted to hang out. Don't you ever want to hang out? Well, forget it then."

He walks away. I make sure he's gone, then glance back at Charlene's apartment window. No sign of life. I walk down Belknap to the corner of Tower Avenue, then walk over to North 16th Street and all the way back up to Grand and Catlin, near the college. Grand Avenue forms a triangle that connects to Belknap, and I follow it to just a few steps from People's.

It is five-thirty p.m. and beginning to get dark. I look up at Charlene's window. A light is on. I walk up the stairs on tiptoes. Why am I being so stealthy? Why do I fear that third step will creak? My heart is pounding. Is it from the climb? From anger at Melvin? Or from anticipation?

I knock. I knock again.

The door swings open as I am about to knock a third time. Charlene is in hair rollers and is smoking a cigarette. Behind her, a porcelain kitchen sink is crammed with frying pans and egg-stained plastic plates from Woolworth's. "Oh, you're back," she squints, blowing smoke over her shoulder. "I guess you could come in."

40

"What do you mean, she reminds you of me?" Peggy says. I have just phoned home, collect, to ask for money for a zoology textbook. Dad agrees to send a hundred dollars "but no more before Thanksgiving," and then says, "Guess who's visiting here tonight."

Peggy gets on the line and tells me the new baby is due in December. "I just know it's another boy," she says. "Can you believe Sean will be three in January? Hey, how's the girlfriend?"

In this phone conversation, she is not the brooding Peggy, the jealous Peggy, the more-mature-than-you Peggy. She is Peggy my friend, the apple cider Peggy, the Clap-the-Whites Peggy. The teasing Peggy.

I try to explain that Charlene is not really a girlfriend, just a girl who is a friend, like my older sister. "I guess because she has two boys also, like you do—or almost do. And she's the same age as you—five days older, I think. And she's very sensitive. I like her."

"Wow. Good thing she's not a girlfriend, huh?"

"What?"

"Never mind. Hey, did I ever tell you I married Richard because he reminded me of you?"

"Yeah. But I don't see it. He's taller."

"It's his eyes. They're like yours."

"They're brown. Mine are blue."

147

"I know, but still."

Ed Boyle signals that he needs to use his phone. "Gotta go, Peggy. Love you."

"Who was that? New girlfriend?" Ed asks.

I am wearing out my welcome at Ed's, and so I am glad when my apartment is ready in mid-September. It is less than a mile from campus. Better yet, it is less than half a mile from Charlene's.

I help Charlene out with groceries. She feeds me Spanish rice and coffee, or hot dogs, or hamburgers, whatever I happen to buy. Inevitably, she launches into a diatribe against the welfare system, against Wisconsin legislators, against Nixon, against the college administration, against all the men who have mistreated her. "Except you," she always adds with a flutter of her lashes. "You're the only decent man I ever knew."

I am not used to being called decent. I am barely used to being called a man.

"I'm serious," she says when I protest. "But we can never get involved, you know. Because of Dusty. He's still in the Navy, and he's still married, but he wants to get a divorce. He says he will, but right now his wife is pregnant."

"Do you hear from him?"

"Oh, sometimes. I saw him last year. No, the year before."

"And he's good to you?"

"Of course. He wants to marry me."

"Then he must be a decent man, too."

"Oh, Jack, don't go trying to compare yourself to other people. You're you. Can I bum a cigarette?"

At the end of September, Charlene needs two hundred fifty dollars for tuition because welfare cutbacks are threatening to end her student entitlement. She says she has a promise from her father for a hundred fifty now and a hundred later, but she needs the whole thing now.

"I can lend you a hundred," I say. "I just got money from my own father. Of course, I'll need it back as soon as you get it from your father."

"Oh! Oh, Jack! Oh, I can't believe you would do this for me!" Her eyes brim with tears. *Doing good deeds is easy*, I think—*especially when it's just a loan.*

One windy, freezing night in October, I babysit her boys while Charlene goes out partying in Duluth with her girlfriend. She comes in at one-thirty, shivering and drunk and playful. She lights the gas oven, opens the door and lifts her skirt to get the most from the heat. We cuddle on the sofa under the glow of a red ceiling bulb. "Turn out the light," she whispers.

The next day, I am hounded by guilt and fear. I am going to Hell. And before that happens, no doubt I will have to support a child, though Charlene assures me it is a safe time of the month. *I'll deal with Hell later*, I think, as I buy condoms at People's Drug.

The affair is over in less than a week. At Cathedral of Christ the King, across the street from where I bought the condoms, I make a tearful confession, impressing the older priest so much that he assigns only three Our Fathers and three Hail Marys as my penance.

I get a letter from Peggy the next day, wondering how the "not-a-girlfriend" is doing. I am too ashamed to write back.

Charlene's father sends her the hundred-fifty, but not the other hundred I have already fronted. "I will pay you back as soon as it comes," she assures me. "In fact, I will apply for a student loan so I can pay you."

The paperwork for the student loan sits on her kitchen table for weeks, gathering jelly and coffee stains. She says she needs more information before she can finish filling it out. I pick up a clean application for her. She loses it.

One day, I buy her five pounds of hamburger, a gallon of milk, and a dozen eggs, and she starts to cook supper for herself and her boys. This time, she doesn't set a place for me. "Jack, I don't want to hurt your feelings, but this food has to last me the rest of the month. Can you just make yourself a peanut butter sandwich or something?"

The next day, I meet her in the student union, as usual. Not as usual, she doesn't invite me to the apartment. "Good news, bad news," she says. "I still didn't get the hundred from my father."

"What's the good news?" I ask.

"I got my period," she says.

41

The post-coital phase of the relationship settles into something frighteningly domestic, mundane, at times quarrelsome. We seem to have explored the limits of our curiosity about each other. She suddenly perceives I am an imperfect man. I am weak, vacillating, overly critical, afraid to commit to a cause or a relationship. She complains she doesn't know what I want or think. Months earlier, my quietness was a virtue, perceived as a willingness to listen rather than talk. Now it's a closing off of the "lines of communication."

Her warts begin to show, too. Regardless of the help I give her in grammar and spelling, she doesn't seem to learn quickly. She can spell the tricky word "receiving" but not the easier word "giving"—she forgets to drop the "e."

One day she answers her door and her hair is short and auburn. "You cut it and colored it," I say.

"Shit, no. The blond hair is a wig."

I don't dislike auburn hair. But somehow I feel tricked.

She cannot understand why her bad credit history should be the reason her student loan is rejected. "As if that was my fault!" she screams.

"As if that *were* my fault," I correct.

"Did I say it was? Am I blaming you?"

She becomes moody. To get her out of her funk, I help her take the kids trick-or-treating, spend a day ice skating with her, and accompany her at songfests at the student union and the Newman Center. On November 13, in gusty, twenty-degree cold, we take part in an anti-Vietnam War march down Belknap Street and Grand Avenue, one of thousands of nationwide marches for Moratorium Day.

"I wish Nixon and Agnew and General Waste-More-Land would show up here today, so I could spit in their eyes!" Charlene seethes, rubbing her chapped hands together. We are jostled on all sides by students wearing black armbands and carrying signs saying *END THE WAR!* and *GET OUT NOW!* Charlene continues ranting, "Oh, and toss in a few Senators, and—"

"Charlene, quit spitting fire all the time, will you?" I say.

"What? You're not on their side, are you?"

"Of course not. But you don't have to go into a big uproar about it."

"Jack, what do you call this protest march, a fucking Tupperware party? It's an uproar! You can't change the world without an uproar."

"It's an organized protest," I say.

"Bullshit," she says.

An elderly priest addresses the crowd from the steps of Cathedral of Christ the King, and I secretly wonder if it's the same priest who heard my confession of fornication. "A popular folk song asks us to look at life from both sides now," the priest is saying. "If killing innocent Asians is right, then how can we know if anything we do is wrong?"

When the demonstrators and the police cars disperse, we gather her boys from day care and I buy us supper at the Patio Café. Then I walk her up to her flat.

"Please don't come in," she says, shooing her kids in before her.

"Charlene, you're upset today. I don't want to leave you like this."

"I'm fine. I'm living in filth while the government is wasting our wealth that could get me out of here. But I'm fine, Jack, OK? Just leave it."

"Leave it? Leave what? You? Let's end our own little war, Charlene. Let's call a moratorium and do something useful. We just came from a march that tried to change the world. Let me at least try to change your little corner of it."

"Change it how? Buy me a loaf of bread and expect me to lie on my back and say we're even?"

"That's not fair."

"Then what do you want to come in for? We already ate."

She closes the door.

I stomp down the stairs, walk back to my apartment as a bitter lake wind nearly blows me over. I try to immerse myself in schoolwork for a change, open my British literature anthology to William Blake's "Holy Thursday" and read: "Then cherish pity, lest you drive an angel from your door."

I force myself to stay away from Charlene. Now there is no excuse for missing classes and getting low grades, but when did I ever need an excuse for that? I have all but given up on zoology and black history, but now I am even missing my literature classes. I am back to 1967 and the months after Gil's death. I sleep late, spend hours at the chessboard, avoid friends and family and schoolwork. My GPA hovers at about 2.1.

A long-haired girl sits under an immense oak in front of Old Main, reading another girl's palm. "Long life line. You'll live into your seventies or longer. You will marry within five years and have three children. The first will be a girl."

I ask her to read mine, just for laughs.

"I see a good marriage, but not yet. Later in life. More than five years. Some problems at first, but they will be straightened out. You will have two or three children. Boys."

"Boys?" Charlene's two young boys immediately spring to mind.

"That's what I see," the girl says.

What am I doing? Why am I listening to this baseless, silly prophecy? If this throbbing in my chest is fear of commitment, why do I let it overwhelm and paralyze me? Why am I not running as fast as I can from the memory of Charlene?

But where can I run to? I am far from home, and my apartment roommate has a live-in girlfriend. Their constant fucking drives me out of the apartment for hours at a time, and I wander the streets of Superior like a homeless man. At the student union, I solve the only problems I can, the artificial problems on a chessboard. I play nameless, faceless opponents for hours at a time, beating them all.

Charlene hangs around with a male student from India. When she has to move out of her Belknap apartment because she can't pay the rent, he moves in with her at her new place. It's OK with me, I tell myself. The only reason I hurt is because Charlene turned me away so suddenly, so impetuously. And because she still owes me a hundred bucks.

"You'll never see it, you know," Ed Boyle says when I drop in on him.

"I think I will," I say. "People are basically good. All people have an innate sense of fairness."

Ed falls off his chair, laughing. Of course he's stoned, but he would have laughed anyway. "All people fuckin take care of themselves first," he snorts. "That's why greed rules the world, the socio-politico-economic continuum is out of balance, and Vietnam is just a symptom of a diseased system that perpetuates world poverty and makes corporations richer than many Third World—"

"Do you take care of yourself first?" I ask.

"Everyone does. We get out of bed, brush our teeth, eat our meals, earn a living. Do you brush Charlene's teeth?"

Sly grin: "Well, I have been known to get her out of bed."

Knowing chuckle: "Haven't you been known to get her into bed as well?"

"Point taken. Not lately, though. I haven't eaten her meals for her, but I've provided a few. And who is earning a living for her? You and me. It's called public welfare, and we're the public that—"

"Here's what I'm saying," Ed interrupts. "If we don't have to do something, we don't do it. Charlene doesn't have to repay you, so she won't."

"You talk about working to end world poverty," I say. "There's poverty right here. I know I haven't done as much as you in the Movement. I haven't gone to as many SDS meetings as you or learned as much about Marx and Lenin and stuff. But haven't I been working to end poverty, one person at a time?"

Ed strokes his beard and lights another joint. "Have you? What have you really been doing? Whether you can admit it or not, the first phase was just leading up to the sex phase."

"I didn't really want—"

"Bullshit. I don't care how Catholic you are. I'm Catholic too, but my cock gets hard. If there was no possibility of sex, you would not have stayed with her. To prove it, imagine if she were not a good-looking woman. What if she were a man?"

"A man would not—well, not many men would—"

"Ask for help? Sure they would. They just wouldn't ask you. They would ask someone who would want to help them because there's something in it for them. You stayed with Charlene because there was something in it for you. After the sex was over, you stayed because you wanted your money back. And now that's the only thing that keeps her on your mind."

Ed takes a long toke, holds it, and offers me the joint. I wave it away.

The next day, Charlene is at the student union with her new boyfriend. They both look embarrassed as I approach. "Charlene, I just wondered if you got the money from your father yet?"

"No," she says, calmly but without warmth. "But I'm still trying to get the student loan. Don't worry, Jack, I'd rather owe it to you than cheat you out of your money."

"I know," I say before I grasp the meaninglessness of the statement. As I walk away, I realize what she believes: if she owes it to me, she isn't cheating me. With an untainted conscience, she will owe it to me forever.

42

The apartment is too small for three, and my roommate's girlfriend doesn't like it there anyway because the tenant down the hall sits in the shared bathroom for thirty minutes at a time, reading the paper and smoking stogies and grunting. In March of 1970, I have the flat to myself, and I put a notice on the bulletin board in the Rothwell Student Center:

> **ROOMMATE WANTED**
> **$30/month + $30 security**
> **Easy walk from campus**
> **Jack Sheedy**
> **1612 N. 16th St.**

I sit by myself at the Center, sipping my coffee and reading Vonnegut's *Welcome to the Monkey House*, when I see Charlene's new boyfriend, Paul Sham, the student from India, reading my notice. I imagine that he comes over to me, sits down across from me. "Excuse me please. You are seeking a roommate, yes?" I imagine him saying.

I'm not concentrating on my book, so I let my mind play out the scene. I stick the school's Jim Dan Hill Library bookmark in the paperback and lay it on the table. I sip my coffee and place the cup directly in front of me. "You're looking for a place, Paul?" I say in my mind.

"Yes, please. I have cash with me."

My eyebrows arch.

"Can I buy you a coffee?" I ask.

"Sure. Thank you, Jack. You are kind."

"Oh, I'll bet you've been told that yourself a few times," I say.

"Please?"

"Cream and sugar?" I say, ignoring his feigned innocence.

"Just black."

"So you don't mind if I ask why you need a place, right?"

Paul Sham is maybe five-foot-one, slightly built, very dark-skinned. I order his imagined presence to fold his hands in front of himself on the table, looking meek, and saying, "Well, as you know, I was staying with Charlene."

"Ah, yes. How is Charlene these days? Cigarette?" *Am I being too David Niven? Nah, go with it.*

A broad but guileless smile, and his hands fly apart briefly, then clasp each other again. "Oh, well, you know."

He is not going to take the proffered Tareyton, so I light it myself. I try this time for a Bogart look, cupping my hands around the match to protect the flame from an imaginary wind. "And how are the boys?" I ask, wagging the match out.

"Oh, the boys. I don't know. Very young," he mumbles.

"Jimmy in first grade now?"

"I think so, yes."

"Good," I smile, knowing there is no Jimmy and the oldest, Jerry, is in kindergarten. "So where are you living now?"

"Here and there. You know, with friends for a night at a time, like that."

I lower my eyes and shake my head somberly. "Rough," I say commiseratingly. "So, I hope you understand, I need to know you can be dependable as a roommate. You have sixty dollars, you say?"

"Yes, sir."

"And these friends you're staying with, they don't want to let you stay?"

"Oh, well, they can't really."

"Oh?"

"Because they're in dorms. And they sneak me in."

"Hmm. I'm trying to be convinced that you'd be a long-term roommate."

Suddenly, he pleads with me. "Jack, don't be angry with me. She dumped me too. She threw me out. She took my money. You and me, we have so much in common. We should be roommates."

Here the imaginary conversation ends, and anyone looking at me would see me smiling. Paul is actually still reading the notice on the bulletin board. Then Charlene joins him, he points to the notice, she slips her hand in his, and they kiss and walk away laughing.

"Hi Jack! Hey, don't say that in an airport, right?"

I twist my head around. Melvin Fairweather is grinning at me, wearing, I swear, the same rainbow pullover he had on when he dogged my steps on my first day back to Superior.

"Melvin, what's up?"

"You and me!" he says. "I'm your new roomy!"

"I don't think so," I say.

"Sure, why not? Hey, I'm out of jail. It was all a mistake, you know. Sure, we were stoned, me and those two kids from Duluth, but I didn't take those museum tapestries. I had no idea, you know, that that's what they were up to, so I stayed in the car like they said. They came running out with these sort of Oriental rugs, I thought, draped over their arms, got in the car, told me to floor it, so I did, and they hid the rugs or whatever they were in my apartment, or most of 'em at least. Did I know what they were? Did I think the cops would raid my place, take the stuff, haul me to jail? Did I know the landlord would kick me out because of it? Hey, I need a place, Jack, and I've got the dough."

What happened to that imaginary conversation with Paul? This is even more unbelievable. Yeah, I heard gossip around campus about a museum theft in Duluth, but I didn't hear who the suspects were.

"So where you staying?" I ask.

"Here and there. Dorms, mostly. They sneak me in. But I can't stay forever."

I am making this up again, I'm thinking. *But it must be happening, because I can't seem to be as cool as my Niven or Bogart personas.*

"And I'm clean, Jack. No pot, no nothing, not for six weeks. Hey, you ever stay up all night reading aloud from *Man and Superman*? What a trip. We'll have girls over, take different roles, Don Juan, the Devil, Ramsden's Statue, and Ana. We're both thinking people, Jack, you and me, we need the intellectual stimulation. Here's sixty bucks cash."

He hands me two twenties and two tens. I shake his hand without really thinking.

43

I could probably get my GPA above 1.9 if I really try, but learning the Latin names of all the bones in the frog seems pointless, and knowing the titles of all one hundred thirty-five chapters in *Moby-Dick* will never get me laid, so what the hell. Melvin, it turns out, is very entertaining, not to mention distracting, keeping me up all night talking nonstop about Shaw, Shakespeare, Bertrand Russell, whatever comes to mind. Speed will do that for you, he tells me. I try not to notice the colorful tapestries of unicorns he hung on the apartment walls, and we never discuss the museum theft.

One day in early April, a cop knocks at the door when Melvin isn't home. He wants to speak to Melvin, but he doesn't say why. He doesn't come in, but he sees the unicorns.

A couple weeks later, I'm in the Rothwell Student Center, when Ed Boyle sits across from me. "Is it true about the cops?" he asks.

"Come again?"

"Melvin just told me the cops raided your apartment and found drugs in the ceiling tiles."

"My apartment? When?"

"This morning, I guess."

I run a mile home in six minutes, but nothing appears amiss. The tapestries are still on the wall. The ceiling tiles don't look disturbed. I haven't seen Melvin for two days.

I walk two or three miles to the police station, steaming mad.

"Did someone enter my apartment without a search warrant?" I demand at the desk.

"Your name?"

"Jack Sheedy, Sixteen-twelve North Sixteenth Street. Did someone search that apartment?"

"Who resides with you?"

"Melvin Fairweather."

A brief hesitation. "Come this way, Mr. Sheedy."

I'm in an interrogation room with three cops. Where is Melvin? When did I last see him? Is he still in school? What did he tell me about the museum theft?

They neither admit nor deny that they have been in my apartment. They're more interested in what I can tell them than what they can tell me.

Seems like Melvin's been breaking parole, and he's still a suspect in the museum theft. And he does drugs, which I already know, though whether he hides them in my apartment I have no idea.

Back at the apartment, I write a letter to Peggy, telling her everything. Melvin comes home while I'm writing.

"I heard the cops were here," I say.

"Who says?"

"You told Ed Boyle."

"He believed that? Hey, love to talk, but I'm like in a rush, man. Gotta see this girl who's hot for me over on Tower Avenue. People think I'm queer, you know? But I'm not, or you'd know it. Hey, maybe I'll score tonight, wish me luck."

"Melvin, Ed says the cops were looking—"

"Later, Jack, this babe's hot."

Peggy wastes no time answering my letter. A week later, I read her urgent handwriting: "Get rid of him! Kick him out! The apartment is in your name!"

I leave Melvin a note and then take a walk. I come home when I see the lights on in the apartment. Melvin is packing.

"I don't blame you," he says, rolling up his tapestries.

"I feel bad, Melvin."

"Don't. I screwed up."

"Tell me the truth about the cops and the museum and the drugs."

"Jack, it's no use. Sometimes, even I don't know when I'm lying."

I spend my last six weeks in Superior without a roommate. On a Saturday early in May, there's a knock at the door. It's Charlene.

"Can I come in for a minute? There's a cab waiting."

Her auburn hair, without the wig, is professionally permed, and she is wearing a new red nylon spring jacket. Her two young boys are with her.

"Uh, sure." I glance out the bay window at the Superior Cab.

"I've got your money," she says. "Or most of it, anyway."

"Oh, OK. Do you want a coffee?"

"I can't stay."

We sit at my folding table, and she puts seventy dollars in the middle of it. "I know I'll still owe you about thirty, but here's this much," she says.

"Well, thanks." I leave the money where it is. I figure it's impolite to snatch it away.

"I got my welfare check, and I returned some books to the co-op, and Paul gave me some money, and—"

"It's OK. I won't keep you. Thanks."

"But then I spent money at the hairdresser's, and I bought a new jacket. And the cab's costing me a lot, too."

"Still, I appreciate—"

"And I still need to get groceries and pay rent. Plus, the boys both need haircuts."

"They look great. Thanks, Charlene, I wish you good—"

"You've been waiting a long time, Jack, I know, but do you think you could wait a couple weeks more?"

She gathers up the pile of money, gathers her boys, and leaves.

44

"Hafta go milk the cows," the stooped old man says. He has pastel blue eyes and wears baggy trousers and a sun-faded, red plaid shirt. His hands are clasped behind him. He is shuffling toward the entrance in the lobby where I am getting ready to vacuum. A tall redheaded aide named Sally takes him by the arm.

I never expected to see Johnny Ryan again. He was old when I was just a kid, and now, twenty years later, he is ancient. It is 1971, and I have just taken a job in housekeeping at the Adams House, a nursing home in Torrington.

"Not today, Mr. Ryan," Sally says. She turns to her companion, a dark-haired aide named Maryanne. "He walked all the way to Coe Park last week," Sally says. "The cops picked him up."

"Johnny Ryan! Is that you?" I ask.

The man who used to plow Mom's garden swivels toward me, and he peers up at me. He is taller than I am, but stooped, so he peers up. "Cows can't wait," he says. "Cows hafta be milked." Sally and Maryanne smile and lead him to his room.

That night, I call Peggy. "He's still living?" she says. "I want to visit him!"

She drives down from Enfield on the weekend, and we sit in the Twin Colony Diner, down the road from the nursing home. At twenty-six, Peggy is still slim and at the peak of her beauty. Her long black hair is accented by a violet bow. Her blouse and skirt are white with violet accents on the collar, pocket and hem. She proudly wears her nursing pin.

"I can't believe we both work with geriatric patients," Peggy says, sipping her Constant Comment. "Aren't they great?"

"Yeah, but so sad," I say, stirring cream into my coffee. "And I don't work with them the way you do, you know. You take care of them personally. I just mop their floors."

"But still. Anyway, why didn't it work out with Charlene?"

This topic is taboo only when Mom and Dad are around. What is always taboo is why I have been living at home with Mom and Dad for a year now, rather than staying in college. I am too ashamed to discuss my 1.75 GPA, my petition to be readmitted, and Dad's refusal to allow me to return and squander another semester's tuition.

"It was just a dead end, for both of us. I thought I was helping, but I guess I wasn't. On the one-year anniversary of when we met, I surprised her with a carton of Kools. She let me in for coffee. Then the phone rings and it's some guy. Charlene says, 'Sure, come on over,' and hangs up. 'Jack, I hate to do this but I have to kick you out. I forgot I promised to meet this guy.'"

"So you left so she could entertain some other guy?" Peggy's eyes widen.

"Basically. Charlene says to wait for her at a diner up the street, she'll meet me in forty-five minutes. Never shows. An hour later I walk back to her place, really pissed. I storm in, raging, shouting, 'Where the hell were you?' No answer. Then I see her nearly passed out on the couch."

"Jack, this is too General Hospital for me. Are you serious?"

"Said she wasn't feeling well but wouldn't let me call an ambulance. So I stayed up all night watching her sleep, hoping she wouldn't die on me."

"What about the guy who supposedly came over?"

"She says he flipped out and ran out of there when she started feeling sick."

"Hmm. There's some information missing, don't you think?"

"Oh, I'm sure. Anyway, after I got back to Torrington, I wrote her a few letters, mostly asking for the money she still owes me. She never wrote back. She finally called a few months ago."

"Don't tell me. She said she still intends to pay you but she's waiting for things to improve first."

"Gee, how'd you guess? Her latest story is that she got a new boyfriend, even got engaged, since she was tired of waiting for Dusty, the

Rhett Butler of her dreams. Then, boom, Dusty shows up, says he's ready to get a divorce and marry her. But he notices the engagement ring on her finger and takes back his proposal, packs up and leaves. Charlene returns the ring to her fiancé. Now she's waiting for Dusty to show up again."

"She's just trying to get by," Peggy says. "And she's still waiting for a prince."

"Yeah, couple years ago, she thought I was the prince. Turns out I didn't have a horse."

"Jack, I hate to say it but you *were* the horse," Peggy says, snorting a giggle. "Anyway, now you're free."

She tears open a packet of restaurant sugar and pours it into her mouth.

"What are you doing? You're diabetic," I say.

"Didn't eat breakfast," she says. "Gotta use up some insulin."

Inside the glass-walled entryway of the Adams House, I say, "Don't slip on my waxed floors."

We walk along shiny linoleum to the room where Johnny Ryan lives with his two sisters. Johnny and Mary are in their nineties, and Bessie is over a hundred. None of the Ryans ever married. They all lived in their rambling farmhouse together, and now they all live in two rooms at the Adams House.

Johnny Ryan is shuffling toward an exit, about as fast and single-mindedly as he used to drive his tractor. He is preparing to round up his cows for the afternoon milking. Never mind that the Ryan farm has long been shuttered, the livestock sold or slaughtered, and the Ryans reduced from ten acres to less than six hundred square feet of living space. "Wrong way, Johnny!" I say, turning him around. "We'll take you back to your room." Peggy kisses him and promises he can go home soon. We deliver him to his room as the aides roll their eyes.

After visiting with the Ryans for a few minutes, I show Peggy one of my favorite residents, a blind old man named Arty Travis who has three fingers on his right hand. Arty, as usual, is restrained in his chair. "Father, son, daughter!" he says to no one in particular. "Free to do as you please! Arty unbuckle George. George unbuckle Ethel. Ethel unbuckle the whole Travis family. Now you're free to do as you please, so Arty unbuckle George. Father, son, daughter! Free—"

"Hi, Arty!" I say.

"Who the hell is that? Now I forgot where I left off! Arty unbuckle— no, Ethel—oh, now I forget the whole thing!" His palsied fingers shake and he is silent for several minutes. I nudge Peggy and put a finger to my lips. Pretty soon he begins again the litany of the Travis family, softly at first, then really getting into it: "Father, son, daughter, free to do as you please. Ethel unbuckle the whole—damn—*GANG!*"

"Hello, Arty!" Peggy lilts.

"Now who the hell is that?"

"My name is Peggy. I just came to visit you. You can be unbuckled soon. Is that all right?"

Arty takes Peggy's hand. His face lights up. He pretends to look at her. "I'm so glad to see you!" he says. "Thank you for coming!" He struggles against his restraints "Ethel unbuckle Arty!"

Peggy looks at me and whispers, "Do you see any aides or nurses?"

I peer out the doorway. In one direction, a woman sits in a wheelchair, barely aware of herself. In the other direction, the floor I have just waxed is deserted and mirrors the ceiling fluorescent lights. "All clear," I say.

Peggy unfastens Arty's restraints, showing the dexterity of a nurse who has done this hundreds of times. "I've got you, Arty," she says. "Let's go for a little walk."

Arty's hand trembles as he offers it to Peggy, who helps him to stand. Together they shuffle past me and into the deserted wing, Peggy clasping Arty's three-fingered hand in one of hers while supporting him around his waist with her other arm. They walk past three or four rooms before turning back, and Arty proclaims, "Now I'm free to do as I please!"

One by one, within the next few months, Johnny, Bessie and Mary Ryan all die. Finally, Arty Travis dies. I don't know how he dies, but I want to picture him maneuvering his shaking hand with the three fingers until he has unfastened his restraints by himself, then standing on weak legs and shouting, "Unbuckled! Unbuckled and free!" before collapsing to the floor, dead but happy.

45

The years roll by. Wisconsin is like a dream that never happened. I have not even a sheepskin to show for it. A set of bookends with the school logo on them is my only proof that I was ever there.

I continue living with my parents until 1973, then move to an apartment. Now I am working at Waring Products in New Hartford, helping to make blenders and other small appliances. I am twenty-seven years old and still doing entry-level work, sweeping floors, pushing hand trucks, supplying parts to assembly-line workers.

One of the workers is a thirty-year-old mother of two boys, not quite divorced. Donna sits next to me while I eat my egg salad sandwich, a slim paperback at my elbow. Her smile is so sweet, it hurts to look away from her.

"What are you reading?" she asks me.

"*One Very Hot Day*," I tell her. "It's by the author of *The Best and the Brightest*."

She simply blinks and keeps on smiling.

Next day, she invites me to her house for a beer, reads my future in her Tarot cards, prepares my astrological chart, tells me I am a Pisces who has big dreams and will realize many of them.

"Do you read palms?" I ask.

"No, I never learned how," she says. "Why?"

"Someone read my palm once. Said I would marry and have boys."

Two years later, in 1975, we are married. She wants to have no one but her kids and our four parents at the wedding, which will be in her backyard by a shrine of the Virgin Mary, performed by a justice of the peace who lives up the road. I try to compromise. "How about if we each invite one sibling? I'll invite Peggy and you invite one of your brothers."

"No. We agreed," she says.

I hand my movie camera to her twelve-year-old son, who keeps it running throughout the five-minute ceremony. Later, when I open the camera, I see I have forgotten to load film in it.

Dad is in semi-retirement and opens a hearing aid store in Torrington, around the corner from his house. While he is phasing out his Hartford office, he asks me to manage the Torrington store. I try it for three years. It takes me that long to realize I have no patience with old, deaf people telling me to speak up, and I quit.

In 1978, now thirty-two years old, I am back doing entry-level work, now as a binderyman in a print shop, cutting and folding and stitching printed materials, then packaging them. This goes on for seven years, and I just get older, my dreams dimmer.

What dreams? The novel, the fame, the riches, the adulation, the autograph seekers, the movie rights. Dreams Donna doesn't share. If I ever glimpse them, I fail to recognize them. One day, an editor of a small publishing house asks me to write a book proposal. I do. He accepts it. Now what do I do? I try to follow through but don't know how. How can I do this? I work sixty hours a week at the print shop, and there are no research facilities nearby. I write the editor and say I can't do it. Say I'm not ready.

Peggy rarely calls me, and I rarely call her. I am too busy trying to keep the mortgage current in Bakerville, and she is too busy trying to keep food on the table for her kids. Her second marriage, to a tall male nurse named Jerry in 1980, started out so hopeful, and now he is gone for days at a time, either with the National Guard or on some fishing trip or another.

So when she calls me on a summer afternoon in 1983, it is a surprise.

"Jack?" Her voice is small.

"Yes. Peggy? Hi, what's—what's up?"

"I just wanted to call and say I love you." I hear organ music in the background, a diva singing "How Great Thou Art" on Peggy's phonograph. "Just a minute," she says. The music stops. "Can you hear me?" she says.

"Yeah, sure. Are you OK?"

"I'm so happy," she says. "Yes, I'm fine, I really am. I just wanted to talk to you. How is your job? How's Donna?"

"The job's OK," I say. "Donna's fine. She's hanging laundry. Michael's married. John just finished high school and has a good job detailing cars. Just a quiet life here, no excitement. Sometimes a little boring."

"You're working in Torrington now?"

"Yeah, at a print shop. Did Mom tell you?"

"Yeah. No, Dad. Both, I guess. They came up to visit last weekend."

"Oh. Everything all right?"

"Oh, sure. They're fine."

Her voice is so small, scared-sounding, like it must have sounded to Dad when she was a first-year nursing student calling him after Kennedy found missiles in Cuba in 1962.

"You, I mean."

"Yeah, I told you. I'm really happy. Jerry's working late. The kids are staying overnight with friends. I guess I'm just lonely."

"How's work?"

"I love the old people. They make me smile and cry at the same time. Does that make sense?"

"You thought the old people at the Adams House were either funny or very sad."

"So many years ago. Tell me about your current job."

"Well, it's OK, I guess. Bindery work, cutting paper on a machine, sometimes doing collating, sometimes using the folding machine. Boring."

"First you said the job's OK. Then you said it was boring."

"I know. But hey. Peggy, first you say you're happy. Then you say you're lonely. Then you say the job makes you sad."

"Happy and sad."

"Exactly. Is it possible to be both at once?"

"I don't know. Sometimes I'm almost both at once. Aren't you?"

"I'm either one or the other, Peggy. Maybe it's your blood sugar."

"Anyway, I just wanted to call. Just wanted to say."

"Yeah. Me too, Peggy."

There is a second of hesitation.

"Come up," she says. "Come up to visit. Just you and me."

"That's a good idea," I say. "I will."

But I don't. After all, we have our whole lives.

Now it is 1984—the year that was once so far in the future that it was the title of a book about the future. I am thirty-eight years old. So far, my writing career consists of a few reports of Winsted Board of Education meetings for *The Hartford Courant* in 1968 and three short essays published in a local weekly newspaper in 1983. My stepsons are grown and out of the house. Donna works in a nearby factory. I plant tomatoes in the spring, mow our little quarter-acre lawn every summer weekend, clean the gutters in the fall, and shovel the driveway in the winter. Then I do it all again the next year.

Now it is March 20, 1985. I have been married nearly ten years, and I am wondering where my life has gone and where it is headed. But it is the first day of spring, and spring always gives reason to hope.

I am nearly asleep when the phone rings. I hobble out to the kitchen, glance at the clock before answering: ten-twenty at night. "Hello?"

It is Pe-Lou, Tom's wife, speaking very calmly but saying things that can't really be true.

"What?" I say. "Oh, no! No!... Where is she?... How did it happen?"

"What is it?" Donna asks when I hang up.

"It was Pe-Lou," I say. "Peggy is in a coma."

46

People get sick all the time, I think as I climb back into bed. *Our family is strong. Dad had a heart attack a couple years ago and recovered. Ann and I take medication for epilepsy and live without restrictions. Mom, Tom and Gerald seem to have nothing at all wrong with them. Peggy's a nurse and knows how to take care of her diabetes. "I can lead a normal life," she told me more than once. I'll call in the morning and see how she's doing. She'll probably be home by then, laughing at the whole silly incident.*

Donna rolls over and goes to sleep. I stay awake trying to remember which of these thoughts I have just said aloud to her, and which ones I only thought to myself. I lie on my back and remember last Christmas. After all the gifts were exchanged at Mom and Dad's house, Peggy allowed me one more: an album of The Platters, featuring one of my favorite songs, "The Great Pretender." I borrowed it months earlier and was trying to return it.

"Jack, just keep it. Merry Christmas," she said, kissing my cheek. Was this to be our final meeting, our final parting, her final gift to me?

I think back to some difficult times Peggy went through during her divorce in the late 1970's. Money was tight, and so for my birthday she sent me a pair of red socks, because, against all odds, I always rooted for the Boston Red Sox. I wrote back: "Peggy, thanks for the red socks and the $10 bill. Love, Jack."

I thought she would know I was joking, but she called me. Her voice was subdued, worried. "Jack, did I really put a ten-dollar bill in there?"

"Oh, no, I was kidding."

"Oh, thank God. I thought I lost my mind there," she said, squeaking out a relieved laugh. "But don't kid like that. I'd put ten dollars in there if I could, but I really can't afford to."

Now I felt bad. What I should have done was to send her some money, even though things were tight in our household as well. Instead, we laughed it off. The following Christmas, Peggy presented me with a single red sock. Inside was half of a dollar bill. "You'll get the other sock and the other half of the dollar on your birthday," she said, and everyone laughed.

The tradition continued for about five years. On Christmas, a sock and half of a dollar bill. On my birthday, the other sock, the other half dollar.

But on Christmas 1984, the tradition was broken for some reason. No red sock, no half dollar. On my birthday, no red sock, no half dollar, no special message. Just a card signed, "Love, Peg."

I realize we are the same age now—thirty-nine. The family has been planning a surprise party for her fortieth. Now what will happen?

I can't even kid her about being the same age. Can't even remind her of old Mr. O'Malley, the chaperone, looking down at us at the dance in Winsted twenty-five years ago. "Is it twins you are?" he said with a wink.

I recall something else Peggy said in that phone conversation in 1983. "It's almost apple cider time," I said. "Remember Mr. Bills and the cider press?"

"Don't remind me of Mr. Bills," Peggy said.

"Why? Wasn't that a good time?"

"You forgot about the tickling."

"No I didn't. What about it?"

"Do you really believe he was just tickling us?"

What else does Peggy remember that I do not? Will I ever get to ask her?

What did Pe-Lou say? Mom and Dad are staying in Springfield to be near the hospital. Peggy's in ICU. Jerry is coming back early from National Guard duty. The whole family is supposed to meet at the hospital tomorrow night.

"Jerry said she was trying to lose weight," Pe-Lou said. "She probably was fasting. She only weighed ninety-eight pounds, but she wanted to lose two more, I guess. Meanwhile, she had insulin in her system and no sugar to use it up. She went into insulin shock."

In the morning, I realize there is no one to call. I don't know where Mom and Dad are staying. My other siblings would be working, unavailable by phone. I go to work in the print shop, cut stacks of papers in half, fold brochures on the Baumfolder, collate and stitch booklets on the saddle stitcher, try to think of nothing.

After supper, Donna and I drive to Baystate Medical Center in Springfield. Mom and Dad are sitting stone-faced in the waiting room outside the ICU. Jerry is huddled in a corner with an old doctor who is solemnly shaking his head. Peggy's three boys are at a neighbor's house. Ann and her fiancé Ed sit next to Tom, Pe-Lou, and Gerald, all silent, all staring at different blank walls.

I hoped Ann would greet me with something like, "Oh, good, here you are, you're just in time! She's been asking for us, let's go see her." But Ann just looks up at me. I realize Ann's black eyebrows are a lot like Peggy's, dark and thick. She looks away again without speaking.

"How is she?" I finally ask Mom.

"Just the same, Jack," she says. "She needs our prayers. Miracles are possible."

I think of Mom's amazing faith. When I was five, she told me I could light a votive candle in church, put a nickel in the tin slot, and say a prayer, and whatever I asked for in God's name it would be granted unto me. "You mean I can make a wish and it comes true?" I said.

"Not a wish. A prayer." Mom always drew proper distinctions. A heavy smoker, she liked to say that tobacco was habit-forming but not addictive—drugs are addictive. When she had a basal cell growth removed from her face, she said, "It was a good cancer, not the bad kind."

"God doesn't grant wishes, he answers prayers. And yes, if you ask for it in God's name, it will be granted."

I put a whole dime in, and the tinkling sound was thinner than the heavy clunk a nickel would have made. I lit two candles and prayed in God's name that I would one day have a Lionel train set like my friend Travers Auburn's, two complete trains on two separate tracks running the length of the cellar, with hills and tunnels and trees and streetlamps and cars and people and buildings that look like a real town. I prayed for a long time, careful to insert God's name every now and then.

That train never came. Oh, I did get one, but it had three cars and one locomotive and ran in a tiny circle. But it was OK, I only paid a dime for it.

I guess it wouldn't hurt to pray again for a miracle.

"Everyone's seen her but you," Ann says. "Want to go in with me?"

I accompany Ann into the intensive care unit. There are cables hooking people to little black monitors that show green LCD graphs. There is a powerful smell of sweetness that sticks in my lungs. Peggy looks like her old Toni doll, lying with her head to one side, her soft black hair smoothed back from her face, her eyes closed tight. But plastic tubes go up her nose. A machine forces air into her lungs with a *WHOOOOSH*, an overloud sound almost like real breathing. I think of the body of Gil Hebberd gurgling almost eighteen years earlier as the police applied the respirator. A body can still make almost lifelike sounds even when the person is missing.

Intravenous tubes pierce Peggy's wrist. There is a tiny instrument attached to her ear, with a light on it. "The technician told me that monitors her blood oxygen levels," Ann says. "Isn't that amazing? Look what they can do!"

"Can they bring her back?" I ask.

"Sure they can!" she says. "Don't you believe that?"

"Yes, I guess so," I say. I have no choice but to believe.

"Let's sing to her," Ann says.

"What? Sing what?"

She starts singing about wandering to the hill, Maggie, like we did in the long long ago, when you and I were young.

But Ann never wandered to any hill with Peggy, never enjoyed a close bond with her sister. Why would she sing about something that never happened?

I guess because it never happened.

We walk back to the waiting room.

Mom says, "I always knew she wasn't mine to keep. I always knew that God lent Peggy to me."

"But she's still here, isn't she? She's just in a coma," I say.

A fat tear fills Ann's eye and rolls down her cheek. I sit next to her and put my arm around her.

Why didn't I think it was real until just this minute?

47

Bob Dylan is on the car radio as I drive home from the hospital. He is singing about a girl who was like a twin, born in spring. The oldies station follows that with The Platters, singing that song from the album Peggy gave me: the one about how real is the feeling of make-believe, pretending the girl is still around.

The next day, there is no change in her condition. The day after that, there is no change. Four days after Peggy slips into the coma, I start writing letters to her. When she comes out of it, I think, she'll want to read them.

"I don't know where your mind is right now," I write: "I don't understand what happens to the mind of a comatose person. Is it still there? Is it still anywhere? Is it floating over your bed, regarding your helpless body in some detached way?"

A week goes by, and I keep writing letters. On March 27, I tell her about my conversation with Ed Steele, the eighty-four-year-old patient at Saint Joseph Residence in Enfield where Peggy works. "Oh, God, what a thing!" Ed said. "They said a Mass for her here the other day, and I made a bargain with—oh, God, I know you're not supposed to do that, but I did, I made a bargain with God. If Peggy got well, I said, I'd go back to the Church. I'm an old Catholic, you know, that hasn't been to Mass or practiced religion for years. But I made a bargain with God, and the

Mother Superior here said I couldn't do that, but I did it; and I went to that Mass, and I prayed for your sister Peggy. God, what a thing!"

A second EEG is performed. The alpha waves are back. Those are the ones associated with thoughts and dreams. Does that mean her brain cells are just shocked, not dead? Is she thinking? Dreaming?

For six days, Peggy doesn't move a muscle. Then she twitches her toes. The nurse says, "Margaret, if you can hear me, stop moving your feet." So she moves them all the more! During visits, Peggy moves her legs whenever Mom is talking to her.

Ten days into the coma, she is on fifty-five percent oxygen. She is on antibiotics for pneumonia. When a technician draws blood from her left arm, she grimaces and pulls her arm back.

Her tongue is mid-line, suggesting no stroke. Her eyes are still closed. When a nurse pries them opens, there is no response to light: her Liz Taylor pupils do not contract.

"I prayed for you at Mass yesterday," I write to her on April Fool's Day, "and afterwards I asked Father Bowler to pray for you. Everyone's doing everything possible to get you back."

I have no choice but to go to Mass. Afterwards, I have no choice but to stuff a dollar bill into the tin receptacle and light a votive candle. The dollar bill makes no sound.

"Remember, it's not a diabetic coma, it's an insulin coma," Mom reminds me. I notice she doesn't say one is the bad kind and one is the good kind. "A diabetic coma is when you have too much sugar in your blood. An insulin coma is when you don't have enough."

She tells me that when Peggy was diagnosed with diabetes as a teenager, her blood sugar was about six hundred milligrams per deciliter, close to diabetic coma. When she was admitted to the hospital in this insulin coma, it was about thirty-seven. Normal is eighty to a hundred-twenty.

"A diabetic coma shouts, 'Watch out! Here I come!'" I write to Peggy. "An insulin coma sneaks out of the closet and pulls the thoughts out of your head. Did you get up at all on that first morning of spring? You said goodbye to the kids as they left for school. You may have gotten up to take meat out of the freezer to thaw for supper. Someone did. You never got dressed. You probably did not take insulin that morning, but it didn't matter: you'd been eating only salads for two days and your blood sugar was dangerously low.

"So maybe you shuffled groggily through the kitchen, nibbled a grape, sipped some water, and tried to think what you had to do that day. Suddenly your thoughts began spilling out of your head, splashing to the floor before you could catch and read them. *'Sleep!'* one thought insisted, the one you could catch and understand. *'Go to work!'* another thought said, but it fell away—was pulled away—before you ever heard it. *'Sleep! Sleep. Slee-eep...,'* soothed your one static-free thought, and you groped your way back to the bedroom, curled up on the bed, and closed your eyes, and the closet door creaked open and out slithered a bogeyman, the insulin coma, pulling the thoughts out of your head, crooning, *'Slee-eep... slee-eep....'"*

48

After two weeks of nearly daily visits to the hospital, I try to resume a normal routine. I work ten-hour days at the print shop, then Donna and the kids and I eat Shake-n-Bake pork chops and watch the news and then maybe "Magnum, P.I." or "Scarecrow and Mrs. King," and then it's dark enough to get ready for bed. Sometimes, when I don't visit Peggy, I find time to write her a letter and save it for when she gets well.

April 5 is Good Friday, and I have the day off. I visit Peggy. Donna stays away, saying she'd rather remember Peggy as the "spunky elf" she used to be.

I stop at Peggy's house first and ride with Jerry to the hospital. The day is bright, the air cool and crystalline, the colors saturated, the sky cobalt. Then we get inside the hospital. The air is hot and sweet-and-sour-smelling, like blood and floor wax and urine.

The tube in Peggy's nose was irritating her, so her doctor ordered a tracheotomy. Now the respirator blows directly into her windpipe through the bore-hole in her throat. Her eyes pop open with each blast of oxygen. Then they close as her body automatically exhales, pop open again with the next blast, seem to look around the room and take everything in.

"It's like she's looking around and sees us," I say.

"If I wasn't a nurse, I'd think so too," Jerry says. "But it's all mechanical. She sees nothing. She's not aware of us. You're just in her line of vision. I wish I could believe otherwise."

"How powerful is believing?" I ask.

"I have immense faith in God," Jerry says. "But I'm a trained medical person too." He pats Peggy's hand and looks at her for a full minute in silence, and I feel like an intruder. Jerry walks to the window and gazes out at nothing.

"I was watching this show on *Nova* last night," he says. "All about the immense delta of the Amazon. If you try to navigate upstream, you get mired down in mud. There is a meandering, ever-changing network of oxbows. You think you're getting somewhere, and suddenly you reach a dead-end after traveling miles. It's a very fertile area, filled with life and possibilities, but it's hard to find your way around it, or out of it. You don't know what to do when you're there. And you don't know how to leave."

Peggy no longer looks like her Toni doll. She looks like she's sixty years old. Her face and hands are bloated. Her teeth have accumulated a foamy white substance. Her tongue lolls around in her half-open mouth, seeming to lick her lips.

The respirator blows her full of air. Her eyes pop open in surprise and gaze directly into mine, pleading with me. What is she trying to ask me?

Nothing. She's not there.

Peggy's doctor comes in and Jerry says, "She doesn't look good to me, Doctor. She was off the respirator for one minute last night, and her blood carbon dioxide shot way up and she had to go right back on. It's like we're in limbo now, or mired in the delta of the Amazon. If she's going to come back as a vegetable, that's unacceptable. Just how long will we be kept waiting? Six weeks? Just how long?"

"I wouldn't be too grave until another week goes by," the doctor says.

Grave. Could he have chosen a worse word? "Ask for me tomorrow, and you shall find me a grave man," said the dying Mercutio in *Romeo and Juliet.*

Jerry and I ride back to Enfield in silence. The weather hasn't changed, but the lustre seems gone from the sun-soaked colors on buildings, billboards, fields and trees. I roll down the window to let the fresh air cleanse me of the smell of the ICU.

Back in Jerry's living room, we flop into easy chairs facing each other. We look at each other for a long time, and finally Jerry gets us each a can of beer and flops down again. We take slow sips.

"What will happen?" I ask.

"It's not good," he says.

"But she seems better in some ways."

"Her brain is badly damaged. It's probably medically irreversible."

"But you have hope, don't you? Miracles happen. And it's Good Friday," I add, as if it means something.

Jerry looks out the window toward the setting sun. "I've seen recoveries I can't explain, as a nurse," he says. "I guess they're miracles if we can't explain them, I don't know. But if someone *can* explain them, are they still miracles? Anyway, I've never known a brain-damaged person to recover fully."

"Does—does Peggy have a living will?"

"No. But we've talked about it. About what should happen. What we should do for each other if one of us—if one of us needs the other one to make a decision."

"So—so you wouldn't hesitate?"

"Sure I'd hesitate," he says. He takes a thoughtful sip of beer. "I had a dream last night," he says, "—the first dream I remember having in three weeks. I dreamed the phone rang in the middle of the night, and it was the police. They told me there had been a murder in the neighborhood—this neighborhood—and that I should get up and shut off all the lights in the house. I got up and looked out the living room window, and I saw two paramedics carrying a body on a stretcher to an ambulance, except I didn't *see* any ambulance. Then I started turning off lights, all over the house. But I couldn't get the kitchen light to go off. I flicked the switch up and down, but the light just stayed on."

49

Joel is Peggy's youngest boy, just shy of nine years old when she goes into the coma. On his birthday, we give him a party at her house. Jerry can't find the birthday candles—doesn't know where Peggy keeps them—so he places two dinner candles on the cake.

"Make a wish," Mom says to Joel, and Joel blows out the candles.

So this is the difference between a wish and a prayer: When you pray, you light a candle. When you make a wish, you blow it out.

How do you know which to choose?

Joel's eyes are wide and bright, and he is laughing as he opens little gifts of Matchbox trucks and polo shirts. His fourteen-year-old brother Ricky looks on but can't seem to smile. His eighteen-year-old brother Sean looks down at his empty plate. Jerry keeps moving about the kitchen, trying to find where Peggy keeps the good coffee cups, the party napkins, the silver cake server.

Mom and Dad lavish all their attention on Joel, and Joel smiles and smiles. I remember the clown costume Dad bought me for Halloween so many years ago—how the mask forced me to smile, how it made Dad howl with laughter. I wonder how Joel can smile without a mask.

50

Monday, April 8, 1985.
Dear Peg,

Happy 40th birthday! You made it after all—barely. We were both 39 for a few weeks. We won't be the same age again until next February 19th.

Mom and Dad saw you yesterday, and you were sitting up in a chair. The nurses had propped you up, but the effect was wonderful, they tell me. Ricky and Joel came in with Mom and Dad and saw you sitting up—with your eyes open! The kids were so overjoyed they called, "Mommy!" and you looked at them. Mom and Dad both believe that for an instant you recognized your kids. Ricky got so excited he tried to call his older brother Sean on the payphone, but he couldn't reach him.

Your eyes remained open for about a minute, Dad said, and then they closed, and you went into a peaceful sleep. Mom said she really believed you recognized Ricky and Joel, but only briefly, and your gaze turned into a blank stare before your eyes closed.

"Why doesn't she talk?" Joel asked.

Dad answered as though you could hear, "The doctors haven't fixed her voice yet, but they will."

If you can be weaned from the oxygen, you can get rid of that tube sticking in your throat, and the hole will heal. Maybe then you can talk.

You're coming back, at least a little. Maybe. At any rate, Dad believes,
you're not dying.
Happy birthday, Peggy.
Love, Jack.

51

For her birthday, Peggy is given the gift of breathing on her own. She is weaned off the respirator and now uses her own power to breathe in the forty percent oxygen they offer her. I make a list of the improvements to her condition since she was admitted less than three weeks earlier: responds to pain; breathes without respirator; smiles, frowns, looks bewildered at times; responds to her children's voices; follows movement with her eyes; sits up in a chair and "passes gas" (Jerry says); has movement of limbs.

I write to Peggy on April 10:

> *The medical people offer no promises, exhorting us simply to "hope." OK, we'll hope, if that's our part to play. And the doctors can doctor. And we can all pray.*
>
> *That is what hundreds of us are still doing. Mom says that if you regain your senses, it won't be a feat of medicine but a result of prayer—a miracle. If I knew too much about medicine, I might not bother to pray; but I don't, so I do.*
>
> *Meanwhile, quit farting in your chair. Have a little class.*

Mom's example of faith in miracles inspires the whole family. But I can't help thinking back to 1967. I needed a miracle the day Gil drowned. It didn't happen that day, but God seemed to be compensating by letting the Boston Red Sox win the American League pennant for the first time in twenty-one years. The Sox finished dead last in 1966 and began the 1967 season one hundred-to-one underdogs to win the pennant—but they won it. Down one game to the first-place Minnesota Twins, with two games to play against them, the Sox came from behind in both games and earned the right to play the St. Louis Cardinals in the World Series. The Impossible Dream Team, as the Sox were called that year, took the Series all the way to the seventh game.

Then, they lost.

Why would God torment me with near misses?

Still, Peggy *is* breathing on her own. She *does* have the use of some of her muscles. She *can* sit up in a chair (and pass gas). If these are not quite miracles—or at least not quite the miracle we're hoping for—at least they give us cause to hope.

A couple days after Peggy's birthday, there seems even more cause to hope. A gastostomy is performed. No more IV feeding. Now food is introduced directly to her stomach through a hole cut into her abdomen. "The nurses say they are going to teach her to walk," Jerry says, and at first I think he's kidding. He is serious. The doctors must have hope—why else would they try to rehabilitate her?

The pictures I took at Joel's birthday party are developed. There is one of Joel blowing out the two dinner candles Jerry stuck in the cake. One candle is already out. One is still lit.

That night, it's my turn to dream. Peggy wakes up. The entire family is gathered around her bedside as she opens her eyes and looks at each of us in turn. "Hi Mom," she says. "Hi Dad. Hi Jack. Hi Ann. Hi Tom. Hi Gerald." She is smiling. It is difficult for her to talk—her tongue gets in the way—but she greets each of us in her clear, calm voice.

On April 25, 1985, I write:

Dear Peggy,

You can't go home again, as novelist Thomas Wolfe said. I just opened a bottle of Coca-Cola and was enjoying the familiar sweet bubbliness tingling my throat. Then I saw a package of Devil Dogs on the counter, a snack Donna picked up today, and something from 'way back 25 years or more ago flashed into my brain. On a hot day in the late '50's I was walking the two miles home from Saint Mary's School, and when I reached Getchell's General Store in Pine Meadow I put a dime in the old red Coke machine and pushed the lever. Then I walked inside and bought a Devil Dog for a nickel from fat, glinting-eyed Mr. Getchell and sat on the cement step to eat it and slug down the Coke.

Devil Dogs were rich, dark, moist devil's food cakes with a creamy white filling. Somehow they went just right with Coke. And for 15¢, you couldn't beat it.

All this came rushing back to me when I tasted the Coke tonight and spied the Devil Dogs. I grabbed the Devil Dog, peeled away the cellophane, and eagerly bit into it.

It tasted like corrugated cardboard.

Some years back, apparently, Borden Inc. ordered Drake Bakeries to change their recipe. And just this month, market research by the Coca-Cola Company prompted them to announce they've decided to change the 99-year-old recipe for making their famous soft drink. Coke will cease to be.

You can't go home again, Peg.

Love, Jack.

52

Sunday, May 5, 1985.

Dear Peg,

Mom just called me with the news: you kissed her today!

And you kissed Dad and Pe-Lou and Joel.

Someone asked you a question, and you nodded your head in response.

And you scratched your nose. You did it by moving your head from side to side while holding your hand against your nose. You have more control of your head movements than of your extremities.

Tuesday night, you recognized me and cried—a brief, hurried sniffle—when I told you I had an article published in the newspaper. You wept at the mention of the names of each family member. And you definitely can see and focus well.

You are in a private room now, out of ICU at last, and soon you'll move to a nursing home in East Windsor where you will get speech and physical therapy. Our prayers are being answered, Peggy.

Early every morning, I hear the sad but hopeful cry of the phoebes in the trees: two syllables, prolonged, as if the birds are calling a name: "Fee-bee..." When you and I were kids, Peggy, I used to hear the same birdcall. It seems it was always when I was by myself,

185

playing in the dirt across the tracks by the Lyn Gas building, early in the morning. "Fee-bee," a lone bird would call, and I don't recall ever hearing a response. Then you would join me in play, and I didn't hear the birds any more.

Now I hear them all the time.

I listen closely now, and I hear your name in the cry: "Peg-gy...."

Two weeks ago I dreamed about you again. I dreamed you were well enough to sit and eat at table with the family. You were smiling broadly, looking around at Mom and Dad and your brothers and sister, happy to be here. This was a dream I had when you were still in a deep coma. It has almost come true.

I thought Jerry was joking two weeks ago when he said, "The nurses are going to teach her to walk." But Mom and Dad brought your sneakers up to the hospital this weekend, and the nurses have gotten you shakily to your feet. Your recovery is under way.

Meanwhile, the birds call your name in the morning, when all is still.

Love, Jack.

53

Sunday, May 12, 1985.

Dear Peg,

This letter will be as short as I can make it, with no fancy imagery or symbolism. No phoebes calling your name in this letter.

You see, Peg, I believe now that some day soon you'll read this letter.

I visited with you for almost two and a half hours yesterday. It was just you and me—Peggy and Jack—enjoying each other's company as much as, or more than, we did when we were best friends as kids. You knew me immediately, and you smiled and stretched your arm out to me, then pulled yourself up to give me a hug. You kissed me.

I asked you questions, and you nodded yes to most of them. You shook your head no once, it seemed. That tube is still in your throat, so you still can't talk.

I told you that a lot of people think you will recover, and I asked you, "What do you think, Peg?" You frowned and sniffled rapidly in and out, briefly, a frustrated sob, and I knew I'd asked the wrong question.

I told you I'd planted a tree for you in my backyard, and you looked into my eyes, shifting your wide gaze from side to side, reading my eyes. "It's a little pine tree," I said, and you beamed from ear to ear.

Sometimes we just sat and stared at each other. You looked puzzled by my silence, so I said, "I can't think of anything to say right now, Peg. It's OK if I don't talk, isn't it?"

You smiled and nodded yes.

We held hands. "Go to sleep if you want, Peg," I told you, and you did, for about fifteen minutes, still holding my hand.

While you were sleeping, a nurse delivered some mail for you, and the sound of her voice woke you up. I showed you the envelope, addressed to you at Room 216-B, Baystate Medical Center, Springfield, Mass. You looked intently at the address, and I asked you, "Can you read that, Peg?"

You nodded!

I opened the envelope for you and removed the card from Dad's sisters, Aunts Eleanor and Margaret from Danvers, Mass. They wrote that they'd heard you were improving. "Atta girl, keep it up," they wrote. "Our prayers are being answered."

Then I let you read it for yourself. It took you a long time, but you read it. At least I think you did. Your eyes moved back and forth, pausing at each word. You were at least trying to read. I don't know how much you comprehended.

I wrote a note to our aunts today, telling them of your good response to the card.

Some day you'll read this letter, Peg.
Love, Jack

54

Wednesday, May 15, 1985.

Dear Peg,

    Congratulations! You can talk!

    Dr. Berger removed the tracheostomy tube Monday, and the hole in your throat was bandaged when Jerry and Joel visited you yesterday afternoon. Joel marched in first, and you said, "Oh,...oh." Jerry, hearing your voice as he followed Joel in, asked you, "Do you know who this is?" You said, "Oh...Joel."

    Oh, Peg, it's a miracle!

    I can't wait to see you again.

    Love, Jack

55

Saturday, May 25, 1985.

Dear Peg,

"You-ell-ah?" you keep saying, over and over, as though you were asking a question. "You-ell-ah? You-ell-ah?"

Sometimes you vary it slightly: "Cue-ell-ah? Joe-ell-ah? You-ell-ell?" Then, in a lower voice, falling chromatically with each syllable: "No-ell-ah." Not a question this time: perhaps a command, a statement, a complaint, a negative conclusion. Always very emphatic.

We could read all kinds of meaning into your utterances, but it is probably babbling. At first you may have been trying to say "Joel" again, as you did so clearly on May 14. But you can't make sense. It's painful to hear your voice, the voice of Peggy, clear as a bell, uttering nonsense syllables.

Twice you've been evaluated for possible acceptance into Mercy Hospital for rehabilitation. Twice you flunked. You were not able to respond. So you will soon be moved to Prospect Hill, a nursing home in East Windsor.

See you soon, Peg.
Love, Jack

56

Wednesday, June 12, 1985.

Dear Peg,

Karen Ann Quinlan died yesterday in a New Jersey nursing home. Karen was 21 when she went into a coma 10 years ago. Her parents fought a historic court battle and won the right to disconnect Karen from life support systems. She was breathing on her own for 10 years.

I last saw you on June 4, in your new habitat, Prospect Hill, a nursing home in East Windsor. You appeared worse. Your latest monosyllable is a prolonged "Ow-ww." Over and over. Your utterances are less distinct. I don't know if you knew us—Mom, Dad, and me—but you kissed us goodbye after our brief visit. Maybe you'd kiss anybody— who knows?

I kissed you, and you kissed me, and I took Mom's arm and we walked away from you toward the elevator. Dad walked behind us, looking down at his polished, black shoes. Mom stared straight ahead, her mouth set tightly. I looked at the dull linoleum floor and wondered why it hadn't been waxed, the way I used to wax the floors at the Adams House nursing home in Torrington 14 years ago, when you visited Johnny Ryan and unbuckled Artie Travis.

Who will unbuckle you, Peggy?

Love, Jack.

57

It is the summer before the 1955 flood. I bite into a juicy strawberry and swallow it. Then I roll out of the hammock and grab Peggy's cat Frosty before she can break the bird's neck. As gently as I can, without hurting either bird or cat, I pull Frosty's jaws open and pull the fat baby robin out. There is a portable hibachi near the willow tree, the kind with a grate that closes over the charcoal pit. I put the bird inside and close the grate.

I keep the bird and hibachi inside the sun porch for four or five days, feeding the robin worms, trying to keep it comfortable with fistfuls of tall grass. When its wings seem stronger, I close the doors and windows of the sun porch and open the grate.

The bird flutters against the windows like a huge moth.

I manage to recapture it and carry it across the tracks, away from Frosty, and set it down under a hickory tree. It sits there. I walk a few steps off. It stays there. I watch it for a few minutes and then leave. An hour later I return. It is gone.

But has it flown? Or has an animal found it and eaten it?

It is the summer of 1967. The turtle at Highland Lake doesn't need saving. Rather, that turtle distracts us from Gil, who is drowning. When I finally find Gil, lying face down in ten feet of water, it is too late. I manage to bring him to the surface, only to lose my grip on him as I try getting his head above water. He slips away forever.

It is the spring of 1985. When I walk out of the hospital after visiting Peggy one afternoon, I inhale fresh air. I look up at the gray brick hospital building, up to where I imagine Peggy's room is, then look out onto the city traffic and beyond, toward a restaurant a block away.

I walk briskly toward the restaurant, enter and find a table by the window, where I can look out at the hospital while sipping coffee. A waitress takes my order—coffee and a muffin—and while I wait, a man enters with a boy who looks to be about eight years old.

The man and boy don't see me. They sit at a table in the middle of the dining area, not looking around at anyone. The man says something in a low voice to the boy, and the boy gets up and walks to the restroom by himself. The man picks up the menu, opens it, and begins weeping silently, as if the menu itself contains some tragic news.

I take out a notebook and begin writing Peggy a letter. "I do not create the stories of my life," I write. "They happen to me, willy-nilly, and all I do is write them down. Perhaps more precisely, they threaten to happen, and either they do or they don't, willy-nilly. The stories of our lives are loosely plotted."

I watch the man for a few seconds. He is still weeping, but no one else seems to be aware of him.

"What if I could choose my endings?" I write to Peggy. "How should your story end? In the real world, we hope you recover. Fictionally, you should die, and then there would be no loose ends. But even more likely is that you'll vegetate for months and years, like Karen Ann Quinlan, gradually curling up like a fetus as your tendons are deprived of exercise."

The weeping man blows his nose. Ashamed of spying on him, I gaze out the window toward the hospital. I cannot imagine why he is weeping. I have no idea what I can do for him.

"We cannot choose how our stories will end," I write to Peggy.

58

On the morning of June 15, 1985, a Saturday, I knock at my parents' door. Mom's eyes are moist as she lets me in. She does not smile. When I hug my seventy-three-year-old mother, all her muscles seem relaxed, but one choking sob erupts from her like a bubble from a stopped-up drain. The embrace lasts a full two minutes. No words are spoken.

Dad is dry-eyed but looks at me only briefly, then at his shoes. He holds a yellow legal pad and consults it. "I think we've called everyone," he says. He looks like he is going to say more, but he just keeps staring at the list and does not move.

The next morning, Dad pulls his Buick into our driveway. I have on my navy blue suit, with a subdued blue tie. Donna wears something blue, I think. Dad, I know, wears his best dark blue suit, with a matching vest and a red-and-blue necktie just peeking through at the neck, tied in a Windsor knot. Mom, her head bowed, sits next to Dad, dressed in—oh, what's the use, she must have been dressed in blue but I don't recall. I know it wasn't black. She wouldn't have been able to stand wearing black.

"John, stop the car," Mom says barely a half-mile later.

"What's wrong?" Dad says, quickly pulling over.

"Peggy loved daisies. There's a whole field of them."

And so all four of us get out of the car and, dressed in our finest clothes, bend over to pick daisies by the side of the road. As I get ready to cross back to the car, Dad says, "Be careful, Jack. Look both ways."

The long driveway to Saint Joseph Residence, where Peggy worked, leads to a parking lot that is crammed with black cars. Tom and Pe-Lou arrive as Dad is parking his car. Ann and Ed immediately park next to them, and then Gerald, his son, Duncan, and his daughter, Heather. The automatic doors part for us at the entrance.

At the end of the foyer is an alcove filled with enormous floral arrangements. Somber men stand at attention, directing people discreetly toward the alcove, where a blue casket lies against the left wall. There's Peggy. She's not thrashing about, not tugging at IV tubes, not babbling "You-ell-ah," not struggling to breathe. She looks like she did the first night we saw her in the coma eighty-eight days earlier: quiet, relaxed, sleeping. Except that she is lying on her back, not curled in a fetal position. And she has no attachments. She is lying there, dressed in a white muslin dress she made herself for her wedding to Jerry five years earlier.

Mom lays the shriveled bunch of daisies on Peggy's casket. They look pathetic beside all the hundred-dollar arrangements. But somehow they look more appropriate. Something Peggy would have requested, maybe.

A week later, I visit Mom. She is sitting on her sofa by a wide coffee table, moving jigsaw puzzle pieces in and out of slots that don't fit. "They say she was all right at two-fifteen that morning," Mom says. "At three-fifteen, she was not breathing. They think she choked on her own saliva, because she had no gag reflex."

"Did anyone try to revive her?" I ask.

Mom squeezes her eyes shut. "Her chart said, 'Do Not Resuscitate.'"

Sitting in the center of the sofa, with a crucifix on the wall to her left and a picture of the Sacred Heart of Jesus on the wall to her right, Mom sobs, "It is so hard to lose a daughter."

A week after that, Donna and I take a tour bus to a whale-watching expedition out of Gloucester, Massachusetts, just for a change of scenery. I have a window seat and stare out for the length of the Mass Pike. Donna holds my hand for a while, then lets it go.

On the deck of the charter boat that's chugging out of the harbor, she stands next to me and we stare back at the waterfront where a statue of a raincoated sea pilot memorializes "They that go down to the sea in ships," from Psalm 107. The statue grows smaller; the land mass is swallowed up;

and then Donna drifts away from me to be with more cheerful company. The boat's engines are cut, and we glide silently in a calm sea, literally in the middle of everything visible. A dark mass moves under the blue-gray surface, erupts to shouts of joy, and shoots a geyser skyward. Just as suddenly, it waves goodbye with its wide, forked tail and is gone. The sea is almost instantly calm once more.

In the fall of 1985, Dad and Mom pay Donna and me a surprise visit. Donna is gracious but visibly annoyed that they have shown up unannounced. "We have some news," Dad says. "Your mother went to the doctor today. She has a lump on her breast."

After they leave, Donna says, "I'm really sorry, Jack. I know this is not a good year for you. Still, they should have called first."

Mom undergoes a modified radical mastectomy, and I wonder if something can be both modified and radical at the same time. I am in the recovery room when Mom is coming out of anesthesia. "How do you feel, Mom?" I ask.

"I'm different than I was," she says, then closes her eyes and sleeps.

In October, Dad and I take a Sunday drive to Puddletown, so we can walk through the woods near our former home. Dad parks his Buick across the abandoned railroad bed at the bottom of the driveway, in the shadow of the same two willow trees I first saw thirty-seven years ago. I try to sing, "There's a tree in Pine Meadow-ww!" but I can't remember the tune or the rest of the words, and neither does Dad.

We walk up the driveway, which is a public right-of-way, and Dad points out the backyard area where the barn, rabbit hutch and chicken coop once stood, before the Flood of '55 tore them away. "That's where the garage was," he says, "the one you damaged when I was giving you a driving lesson a few weeks before the flood took the rest of it."

"I remember," I say. "Mr. Rood came over and patched it up. All for nothing."

We walk over to George and Minnie Hough's cellar hole. Thick pipes protrude from the rock foundation, and thirty-year-old trees sprout from the cellar floor. "After the flood, this hole was filled with water for months," Dad says. "While you kids and your mother were staying with the Doyles in Simsbury, I stayed in our house, shoveling mud out of it. I got so filthy, I resorted to taking a bath right here, in the slightly less filthy water of the Houghs' cellar."

I look back toward our old house and point to a window on the second floor. "That's where Minnie and George crawled through," I say.

"Yes. We very nearly were not available to save them. I almost took you kids out of the house before the water got too high. If I did, Minnie and George might have died."

"Miracles are random," I say.

He seems to gaze straight through our old home and says something so softly I don't catch it. It sounds like, "We rented a chair." I know that can't be right, but before I can ask him to repeat it, he says, "Let's walk to the spring."

I take his hand and cross the street. "Look both ways," I tell him. We hike into the woods along Mr. Bills's old tractor trail. We find the reservoir he built some fifty years ago for the spring that once fed the vat where he used to dunk Peggy and me. The ramshackle wooden structure is nearly hidden by fallen birches and old hawthorns, and not much bigger than a doghouse. Its peaked roof is covered with tarpaper that is ripping away from rusty nails. One wall has collapsed into the reservoir, shallower than it once was, and now filled with stagnant water. The conduit that led from this reservoir has long since collapsed, and the spring feeds no one.

We walk back to the driveway and up to the rebuilt sun porch. Dad knocks on the door to our old house, and Mrs. Bowdoin, a longtime family acquaintance who now owns the house, greets us with a smile. "Would you mind if we looked around at our old home?" Dad says.

It feels so much smaller now. I can stand on tiptoes and touch the ceiling in the kitchen—the same kitchen we had installed after the flood, with the curved Formica counter, the electric range, the built-into-the-wall electric oven, the cabinet doors where Tom gashed his thigh when he jumped off the counter in the summer of 1959. The old KitchenAid dishwasher is gone, but a newer model is installed in its place. Dad runs his hand along every surface. He paces the length of the living room, gazing at the walls, the ceiling, the mantelpiece, as Mrs. Bowdoin and I watch in silence. "I love this old house," Dad whispers.

"I know you do," Mrs. Bowdoin says.

Upstairs, Dad walks through the boys' former bedroom, the master bedroom, Ann's bedroom. He glances at the closed door to Peggy's old bedroom and does not ask to step inside it. In Ann's bedroom, he opens a closet door and points to the flue pipe. "My mark is still there," he says.

A horizontal line is drawn in pencil on the pipe. Dad asks for a yardstick and measures the distance from the floor to the mark: twenty-five-and-a-half inches. Underneath the line, again in pencil, is Dad's handwriting: "High water, August 19, 1955."

In the yard, Dad tells Mrs. Bowdoin where the drywell is. He tells her how far out he'd dug the trench where he'd buried the Orangeburg pipe, where the right angle turn is, where it ends near the old railroad bed.

"You did a lot of work," she says.

"Oh, I was strong as a bull," Dad says.

Dad buys me a lunch and then drops me off at my house. Donna trudges up from the cellar with a basket of dried laundry. She brushes past me without a word. "What's wrong?" I ask.

"Nothing."

"Something is."

"I've talked to a lawyer," she says. "The papers will be served this week."

59

"Of course you can," Mom says. "You can have your old room," Dad says.

"I'll pay board," I insist.

The irony is that Donna and I now work at the same place, a direct marketing company in New Hartford, for the first time since before we got married. But we no longer commute together. We try to be civil in public and private, but we are both hurt. The strain of Peggy's illness and death was more than our marriage could bear. My long absences while I was at Peggy's bedside or visiting my parents or siblings made Donna feel neglected. In turn, I felt a lack of warmth from my wife when I needed it most.

The divorce goes quickly. The house, which was always in Donna's name since her first divorce, remains her property. She does not attempt to impose any financial obligations on me.

That sounds like a nice, clean break; but illness, death and divorce are never tidy. I am still in the middle of moving out when she changes the locks. She has all my remaining personal effects piled sloppily in the basement and watches me with her arms folded as I load them into my Subaru wagon. She paints my former den pink even before my typewriter is removed.

After her mastectomy, Mom's arm is in a sling, and she now also has painful, crippling arthritis. Dad has to help her into the tub, bathe her, help her out of the tub, and dry her off.

Mom and Dad try to sympathize with my marital plight, but they are still reeling from Peggy's death and Mom's illnesses. Most of their "sympathy" is in the form of ex-wife bashing. Mom says, "Well, she never was very ambitious, was she? What is she, just a charwoman, cleaning bathrooms at that factory?"

One morning Donna calls me up to ask if I would give her a ride on my way to work because her car broke down. I agree, and Dad launches into a tirade about the nerve of that ungrateful guinea who practically threw me out of the house. I scream at him to mind his own business about the woman I married, and Dad slinks away, ashamed at his own comments. Mom is quiet for a minute, then says, "He wasn't thinking. He would defend me the same way you defended her, if it came to that."

The final divorce decree is dated February 19, 1986, the day I turn forty years old. It is the only birthday present I receive. No one sends me a birthday card. No one throws an old-fart, over-the-hill party. The sun sets, and not even my parents say anything more than "Happy birthday." At night, I drive downtown to the Pumpernickel Pub and buy myself a bloody mary. I raise the glass to myself and celebrate the fact that I am forty years old and alive and conscious, able to say more than "You-ell-ah." Then I buy myself another bloody mary.

A loud, wizened woman staggers in, announces to all that she is "back from the dead!" She tells the story of how her drunk-driving accident left her in a coma for six months while the doctors fed her alcohol intravenously because her body needed it. "Now I'm back, and I can drink the good old-fashioned way!" she shouts, and falls off her stool.

What kind of miracle is this? Peggy's coma leads to her death, and this drunk bounces back and breathes the air Peggy should be breathing.

The months drag by, and Mom gets more and more disabled. She has a bell by her bedside, a round service bell like in hotel lobbies, and she rings it when she needs help getting to the bathroom. When Dad doesn't hear it—he's had stapedectomies on both ears and his hearing is still not good—I get up and help her. I feel as if I should never leave the house, but I know I should not let myself become trapped.

I meet a woman and try to gather the courage to ask her out, but my social skills are rusty. I mention that I am living with my parents. "What? Shame on you! At your age? Move out," she says.

Suddenly I lose it. "Why?" I shout. "They're getting old. They need help. I'm not going to leave them alone. Mind your own fucking business! Want to see a movie?"

I shuttle Mom and Dad to Mass on Sundays and try to feel something from the service. I enjoy singing the hymns, and I enjoy some of the homilies, but I just can't buy into the whole magic show any more. It's just as easy to believe that Peggy never died; that blind old Ed Steele didn't weep as he groped his way to her blue coffin at Saint Joseph Residence; that a never-ending line of nurses and aides and patients and doctors and family members and Peggy's friends did not shuffle past us, sobbing like babies; that an unseen cicada, high in a tree in New Saint Francis Cemetery in Torrington did not begin buzzing as I helped five other pallbearers carry the coffin to the deep hole.

I stay with my parents for nearly two years. In the summer of 1987, I take a second job delivering pizzas. While waiting for a pizza to be packaged, I see a personal ad in a local flier. I write to the post office box. The next day I get a letter from the woman who placed the ad. I drive to her house and she runs out the door and nearly knocks me down with a desperate hug. She practically drags me inside the house and tears her clothes off. Later, I go home and write her a letter saying I don't think a relationship will work out.

She writes back and says that's OK, and that I should check out the latest personal ad in the current week's flier. "This one's a writer, like you. I think she's right up your alley."

I pull the flier out of my wastebasket. The ad says: "A nice woman, divorced, in her 40's, a writer. Loves cats. Looking for a man of intellect and integrity."

I write to her at midnight. I drop the letter in the post office at six in the morning. At six that night I get a call at the pizza place.

"This is Nice Woman," says the voice.

We meet two nights later at a restaurant. Her name is Jean Sands, a pen name that she made her legal name a couple years earlier, to rid herself of the last ties to an ex-husband. She writes poetry. She wants to write prose. She loves to read.

"What are you reading now?" she asks me.

"*Searching for Caleb*," I say. "It's by the author—"

"—of *The Accidental Tourist*," she finishes. "Anne Tyler. My favorite author!"

A sort of miracle is beginning. One that Jean and I can see, even if no one else can.

60

Jean sees me popping Phenobarbital and Dilantin three times a day and says, "I can't believe you never got your epilepsy reevaluated." She makes an appointment with Ann's neurologist, who determines that, since I have had no seizures in twenty-three years, I can be weaned off the medicine. More than two decades after that, I am still seizure-free, medication-free.

Sometimes, things are just that simple.

Jean and I get married in 1989. Peggy's oldest boy, Sean, now twenty-two years old, records the event with his video camera. This time, there is film.

Family members stream down the aisle, past Sean's camera. Dad wears his three-piece suit with a red carnation in the lapel. He smiles into the lens. Next to him, Mom, hobbling but smiling, wiggles her fingers at the camera. There is a gap after Mom, as though someone should be behind her, and then my siblings follow: Ann, flanked by Ed; Tom, Pe-Lou and their fifteen-year-old son Doug; and Gerald, now divorced, with his twelve-year-old son Duncan and ten-year-old daughter Heather.

Watching the video years later, I realize my parents and siblings are more than bit players in my life. Longsuffering Mom grew up a virtual orphan: her mother dead when she was six, her father unable to care for her. Despite that, she earned her RN and was a public health nurse by the time she met Dad in 1943. Dad, a Boston College graduate with an unmarketable liberal arts degree, sold insurance door to door before moving from Danvers to Torrington, where the factory jobs were. After Pearl Harbor happened just a few months after he arrived, he tried to enlist in the Army, but his hearing problem prevented it. He married Mom in 1944 and opened a hearing aid dealership in New Haven. He later moved the office to Hartford, where he was a respected businessman who never quite struck it rich.

Ed makes a face into Sean's camera lens, and Ann playfully slaps his wrist. Above the din in the church, she says, "Happy wedding, Jack and Jean!" and walks out of camera range. She is forty-one years old, a social worker with the State of Connecticut, a woman who is sharp and sensitive and knows how to size up people quickly and accurately. "Peggy and I had issues we never resolved," I remember her telling me after Peggy died. "That's what I miss about her—the same thing I missed when she was alive. That we were never the kind of sisters I wanted us to be."

Tom sees the camera and breaks into a mock grin, all teeth, as though a simple smile would be too commonplace. "Hey!" he says. "Happy happy!" Pe-Lou rolls her eyes. Tom was just a pesky younger brother who loved cars as a kid, but when he tried his hand at operating a service station in Torrington in the 1970's (Tom's Atlantic), he flattered me by asking me to teach him bookkeeping methods Dad taught me. Now, Tom manages an auto parts division at a major Connecticut dealership. "I worshipped the ground Peggy walked on," he told me after she died. I had no idea how close they were.

Gerald is flanked by his kids, whom he adores. He looks into the lens and says, "Hi Jacket!" It was Peggy's sobriquet for me, now used by the rest of my siblings. "Hi Jean, too!" he adds. Gerald was closest to Tom growing up and remains so. Now thirty-nine, he manages an auto parts store in Bristol. When Peggy was dying, I drove Gerald to the hospital one night. He knew she was dying—or at least not returning to life. Either scenario was more than I ever admitted to myself. On the way home, he broke down in tears and said, "Oh, Jack, she was such a sweet person!"

I recalled Hamlet's words at witnessing Laertes' rage at Ophelia's funeral: "What is he whose grief bears such an emphasis?"

Why was I surprised at the depth of my siblings' grief? Who ever said that I alone was entitled to mourn her?

Jean and I buy a house in Harwinton. From the living room window I can see Charlotte Hungerford Hospital in Torrington, where Peggy, Ann and I were born. We are two miles from Mom and Dad's home.

One March morning in 1990, Dad takes Mom for a drive and they stop outside our house. They don't get out of the car. Are they still thinking of the frosty reception Donna gave them five years earlier when they arrived uninvited to announce that Mom had breast cancer? "We just wanted to drive by," Mom says from her passenger seat. "We won't get out. I don't think my legs can climb the steps anyway."

Jean and I watch them drive away. "I think she is saying goodbye," Jean says.

I see Mom one more time, on the last day of March. She is confined to the living room sofa, where she sleeps, where she eats when she can, where she sits all day struggling with emphysema and other ailments. It is the spot where she has spent most of her time in this house: watching television, playing solitaire, assembling jigsaw puzzles. From here, she watched televised games of her beloved, but heartbreaking, Red Sox. From here, on this day twenty-two years ago, she and I watched LBJ announce that he would not seek re-election. The next year, she and Dad and I watched Neil Armstrong take one giant leap for mankind. "I never thought I would live to see this day," Dad said then. A human being was as far away from home as anyone in history had ever been. Now my mother is anchored to this tiny sofa in this tiny living space in this small house in Torrington.

"I think this is the beginning of the end," Dad whispers to me in the kitchen. I kiss Mom goodbye, tell her I'll see her later.

The next day is April Fools Day. But when the phone call from Charlotte Hungerford Hospital comes, Jean and I know it is not a joke. We meet Dad in the emergency room. "I was helping her to the bathroom," he says. "She stumbled. Just collapsed. Didn't say a word. She was too heavy to lift. I went outside, walked to the neighbor's house. They came, tried to revive her, but they couldn't. She died on the living room floor, right next to the sofa."

I want to look at her body, even though Jean tells me I shouldn't. Mom's eyes are still open, still fluid-filled and clear, but staring into a corner. There is a tube sticking out of her mouth, a remnant of some paramedic's life-saving attempt. Jean squeezes my hand, tells me we should leave.

I can't seem to cry. I remember my nephew Joel's apparent cheerfulness when his mother died nearly five years ago, and I hope the mask I am wearing does not look like Clarabell, or like Howdy Doody's wooden smile.

At Dad's house, Ann, Tom, Gerald and I help him compile the list of people to call. He adds the names to the yellow legal pad he consulted when Peggy died. He stares at it. "I think that's everyone," he says.

He lays the legal pad on the Hitchcock table and stares opaquely out the dining room window. "We've had a good life," he says, and I'm not sure if "we" means him and Mom, him and his kids, or all of us. "We've had our share of troubles, but we've been granted our share of blessings."

The rhythm of his speech stirs a memory. I recall the walk he and I took a few years earlier to the old homestead in Puddletown, when I said, "Miracles are random." I thought he replied, nonsensically, "We rented a chair." Now I know what he must have said:

"We are granted our share."

Some details are too trivial to remember, but I do anyway. The medical supply company charges by the day for the rental of Mom's breathing machine, and a parishioner from Mom's church offers to return it. Dad forgets to deliver Mom's dentures to the funeral home, and I hand them to the funeral director in a Ziploc Sandwich Bag. No one knows what to do with Mom's soiled clothes the ER nurse gave Dad, and I take a whiff of them and toss them in the garbage.

As at Peggy's funeral, I am amazed at the throngs of mourners. Did anyone not know my mother?

Later, at the reception at the homestead, my father surprises everyone by singing his favorite Harry Lauder song, "Keep Right On to the End of the Road." He explains that Harry Lauder wrote it after the death of his son, a reminder to himself that

When you're tired and weary, still journey on,
Till you come to your happy abode,
Where all you love and you're dreamin' of
Will be there, at the end of the road.

The end of Dad's road comes seven years later. In 1996, Tom and his second wife, Fran, take Dad into their house in New Hartford—the house that once belonged to Dad's good friend Bill Miller, who accepted a beer from Dad after the Flood of '55. By now, Dad is weak with Parkinson's and colon cancer. He lives with Tom and Fran for ten months, then goes into a nursing home in May of 1997. "Just let me die," he says when the morphine isn't strong enough. But one day in June, he seems determined to conquer his lack of appetite and allows an aide to spoon-feed him. He eats so fast he nearly chokes. When he stops coughing, I ask him if he's all right.

"I'm fine," he manages to whisper.

I believe—because I want to believe this—that they are his last words.

Two days later, it is Father's Day and also the twelfth anniversary of Peggy's death. Dad is moribund—a word he would have used, which means he looks like an old dog that has been run over by a cement truck and is lying on its side and gasping its last breaths. I think of Linda Loman's speech in Arthur Miller's *Death of a Salesman*: "He's not to be allowed to fall into his grave like an old dog. Attention, attention must finally be paid to such a person."

At some level of consciousness, Dad must know what day it is, and he decides to hang on. Two nights later, Tom and I visit him. Dad is breathing through his mouth while a male nurse moistens his palate with a wet Q-tip. "We've taken care of everything, Dad," Tom tells him. Dad cannot respond, and Tom wipes his eyes and leaves the room. I stay behind long enough to say, "I love you, Dad. See you later." I kiss him on the forehead.

In the parking lot, Tom gets into his silver Ford pickup and watches me wipe grime from the headlights of my blue Tercel. "What are you doing?" he asks.

"Dad taught me this," I say. "It helps you see better in the dark."

The call from the nursing home comes to me the next morning. I call Tom, tell him to call Gerald. I call Ann. We all meet that afternoon at the funeral home to agree on arrangements. I want to ask Dad where he put his yellow legal pad, but he's not here.

"When I was eleven or twelve," I say in my eulogy, "Dad bought me a heavy, sealed-beam, nine-volt, Eveready lantern—the kind you carry like a suitcase—to use on my Boy Scout camping trips. On dark and cloudless nights, Dad would take me outside, carrying the suitcase filled with light. He would show me the stars, aiming the powerful beam high into the sky. 'You can't see the stars in the daytime,' he said. 'You can only see them in the dark. It's a mystery.'"

I pack Dad's belongings into cardboard cartons and layer the four flaps over one another, the way Mr. Bills used to do with his boxes of nails. The first three flaps are easy. *But how do you get half of the last flap under half of the first flap without bending the cardboard?* There's a trick: raise the first flap ever so slightly but not so high that it pops every flap loose;

then, very carefully, bend the final flap under it and flatten them all. Some mysteries can't be solved, but some can.

We hold an estate sale at Tom's house, selling off items none of us has room for. Mom's cracked Hummel figurines go for twenty-five dollars. Brass horsehead bookends go for ten bucks. A christening gown that may have wrapped infant Peggy in 1945 is marked down from priceless to best offer.

The rest of the useful stuff is divided as evenly as we can manage: furniture, kitchen appliances, tools. I get the family photo albums, and I scan each photo and give them to my siblings on CDs.

Within three months of Dad's death, his remaining two siblings die in Massachusetts, leaving us without a living Sheedy ancestor. Barely five years later, our last McElhone ancestor, Mom's sister Louise, dies at age eighty-seven. In January of 2003, we become the older generation.

A month after Aunt Louise's death, I get a phone call from a man named Lenny in New Jersey. "I saw your Web site on the McElhone family," he says. "You had an aunt named Jane Nesbitt, who was born a McElhone."

"Yes," I say cautiously.

"Um, did she or anyone in your family ever mention anything about Jane McElhone having a baby girl in Paterson, New Jersey, in 1925?"

"Are you sure you got the right McElhone?" I say.

"The woman was named Marilyn. At least, that's the name her adoptive parents gave her. She died several years ago, unfortunately."

"There was no Marilyn in my family."

"She was my mother," he says.

"Aunt Jane had eight kids, my cousins the Nesbitts. In fact, she called them the Eight Snuffs, meaning Eight is Enough."

Lenny sighs, apologizes for taking my time. We say goodbye.

But wait, I think, moments after hanging up. *Paterson? In my grandfather's 1938 obituary, it said he had lived in Paterson. My family research showed that three of his kids lived with him after my grandmother died in 1918: Tom, Louise and Jane. Was Jane in Paterson in 1925?*

I don't have Lenny's phone number. I don't have his exact address. I Google him and finally locate him.

I write to him, tell him what I know, offer to help him research information about his possible grandmother, my Aunt Jane. He sends a black-and-white photo of his mother: it could be a photo of my own mother.

I enlist Ann's help in the research. There is not much to learn about Aunt Jane in the 1920's, but in the early 1930's she worked at a department store and met her future husband, Jim Nesbitt. They married in 1936 in Paterson, moved to upstate New York the next year. Their first of eight children was born in 1937.

In April, Ann and I drive to Paterson to meet Lenny, and the three of us pore over Paterson city directories at the library, discovering all the addresses Jane, Tom, Louise and their father Alexander, my grandfather, lived at from 1923 to 1936.

Lenny drives us to some of the locations, including an apartment where they all lived for several years. The once-Irish neighborhood is now Hispanic. Ann knows some Spanish and asks the couple if we can see the apartment our grandfather once lived in, and they are happy to oblige.

Still, there is no smoking gun. No absolute proof that Jane McElhone gave birth out of wedlock in 1925 to a child who would become Lenny's mother. A child who could have been a cousin I never knew, a half-sister my Nesbitt cousins never realized they had.

But New Jersey law allows Lenny to uncover the original birth certificate of his mother. Marilyn Bradley was originally named Jane McElhone, the same name as her own mother. The birth date is May 28, 1925. The mother's address is the same one Ann, Lenny and I visited in Paterson. The mother is white, aged nineteen at her last birthday, and she was born in Danbury, Connecticut.

My Aunt Jane was born on March 26, 1906, in Danbury, Connecticut. No other Jane McElhones were born in that city, ever.

Lenny shows us another photograph of his mother, this one in color. Her eyes are bright blue.

What did anyone know and when did they know it? If Mom knew, she never confided anything to us. Aunt Louise, who died weeks before Lenny first called me, once lived at the same address in Paterson where Jane lived. If anyone knew, she did. But she never breathed a word of it to us.

"Nothing's worse in the world than to lose a child," Aunt Jane told me when I was ten. *Unless it's having to give one up for adoption because you're nineteen and unmarried and Catholic in 1925*, I think.

I recall the clear, bright eyes of Mrs. Baxter at Bruce's funeral, her stoic, Protestant, stand-tall manner, her attempts at humor that could not quite hide unbearable grief. I hear again the sobs of Mr. Hebberd at Gil's funeral, his despairing wail about his "great loss." And I see Mom, pug-chinned, mouth clamped tight, trying to fit a puzzle piece of the sea where the sky should go, and saying, "It's so hard to lose a daughter."

And then I recall what happened to them all. Aunt Jane had eight more kids; Mrs. Baxter was more active in her community and church; Mr.

Hebberd found a way to put me at ease at his own son's funeral; and Mom became a lay reader at Saint Francis Church, got active at Women's Club meetings, rejoiced when Jean and I got married.

Jean urges me to put my writing talents to better use. We both become regular contributors to the arts and entertainment section of the local paper. At the direct marketing company where I work, I move from bindery and printing to computerized typesetting and then to copywriting, writing ad copy for the catalogs. I take advantage of a company program and go back to college, fulfilling my long quest for a bachelor's degree in 2003.

A year later, the company closes, laying off everyone. I see it as an opportunity, but finding a decent job at age fifty-eight is difficult. The opportunity that does present itself could not have been scripted by any author of fiction: Nineteen years after Peggy's death shook my faith to its foundation, I am a writer and photographer for *The Catholic Transcript*, the newspaper of the Catholic Archdiocese of Hartford, the same newspaper that forbade us from seeing "Butterfield 8" so long ago.

On a recent assignment, I visit Saint Joseph Residence in Enfield, the nursing home where Peggy worked and where her body was laid out. Here is the alcove where her blue coffin lay with the withered daisies we picked by the side of the road. There is the corridor where hundreds of resident mourners lined up with canes and walkers and wheelchairs. And here is the chapel where my voice cracked on the high notes of "How Great Thou Art." I haven't been here since she died.

It is March 20, the anniversary of the start of Peggy's coma. It is too early for a heat bug to warn me of its sting. But it is not too early for the first phoebe of the year, which sings Peggy's name the minute I walk out the door. I look up into the just-budding branches of the maples on the nursing home's grounds. Like the heat bug, phoebes are hard to spot, and I don't see it.

But it still sings.

Acknowledgments

Some of the material in these chapters first appeared in whole or in part as articles or essays in the following periodicals and magazines. My sincere appreciation to the editors:

The Litchfield County Times (Aug. 9, 1985; June 15, 1990; Aug. 23, 2002)

The Register Citizen (Aug. 19, 1985)

Northeast (Jan. 18, 1998)

The Hartford Courant (June 16, 2002; April 10, 2004; Jan. 29, 2012)

My personal gratitude to those mentioned in this book—whose names, for reasons of privacy, may have been changed. Without them, there would be no story.

Thanks also to a team of friends and astute critics whose guidance was invaluable: Adele Annesi, Janette Bornn, Nancy McMillan, Joseph Montebello, Mary Carroll Moore, Kristine Newell, and Lois Watts. Special recognition goes to my wife, Jean Sands, whose good editorial eye enriched the manuscript, and who supported me through the often difficult days of writing, revision and final editing.

Finally, endless appreciation to my family members, living and passed on, who are the source of love and memory.

18416904R00112

Made in the USA
Charleston, SC
02 April 2013